REX INGRAM

Master of the Silent Cinema

REX INGRAM

Master of the Silent Cinema

Liam O'Leary

BFI PUBLISHING

This book, co-published by
the 12th Pordenone Silent Film Festival
and the British Film Institute,
is a reprint from the 1980 edition
by The Academy Press, Dublin.

Le Giornate del Cinema Muto
ISBN 88-86155-01-8

British Film Institute
ISBN 0-85170-443-3

Foreword to the New Edition

I have fond memories of this book being written. Liam O'Leary, whom I met at the British Film Institute when I first joined as a schoolboy in the 1950s, filled my head with stories of Ingram, as adults of an earlier age filled boys' heads with stories of Drake and Magellan. We lived in the same part of London, and we would often travel home together on the underground, Liam regaling me with the astonishing facts told him by his latest Ingram discovery. He showed me original drawings by the great director, who was a brilliant artist, and displayed the letters he had written his family from school.

The only Ingram available in England then was *The Four Horsemen of the Apocalypse*, and I remember being allowed to borrow a 16mm print, and taking it one winter's night to my parents' home in the country. This was before the age of television, when a film show was an event, and the picture had tremendous impact, even though it was projected on a living room wall. My parents told me it had been the film they had seen on their first evening together.

Liam eventually went to the United States and met Alice Terry and several of the Ingram technicians. When I went out, a few years later, he gave me their addresses and I did the same thing. At last it was possible to see more of Ingram's work, by borrowing prints from MGM through the American Film Institute, with whom I was working. I recall how nervous Alice Terry was to see herself in *Scaramouche*, and how relieved she felt when the picture held up so well. How she and cameraman John Seitz recalled hilarious incidents from the Ingram days. This became a regular event, and I noticed how frank were the Ingram crowd — which now included editor Grant Whytock and cameraman Lee Garmes — about the wildly varying standard of the pictures.

They were full of gratitude to Liam, the first historian to show anything more than passing interest in Ingram, and when I left, Alice Terry gave me a pile of stills and drawings with strict instructions to give them to Liam — one of the more difficult tasks of my life.

Despite the fascinating story he had to tell, Liam found it hard to find a publisher, and when the book appeared it received no worthwhile publicity and disappeared again, as Liam mentions in his letter on the following page, along with the publisher. He was delighted to know that it was to be reprinted with the support of the BFI, and it is very sad he was not able to see the book reborn. We all owe him an enormous debt — as we all owe Pordenone a debt for giving new life to the fascinating and provocative work of Rex Ingram.

Kevin Brownlow

Notes and Amendments

FOREWORD. This can stand unless you want me to write a new one for the Italian
edition.

CHAPTER 1. Page 19 . 5 lines from the end. Cut out " curious mono-rail" and
use " the famous West Clare Railway celebrated in the songs of
Percy French"

CHAPTER 2. " Newhaven Massachussetts should be " New Haven , Connecticut" Page 23.

CHAPTER 3. O.K.

CHAPTER 4. O.K.

CHAPTER 5 Illustration on page 67 should be captioned " Alice Terry in her
first starring role. With Joseph Kilgour. "

CHAPTER 6. Page 99. 2nd paragraph. Colman should be Coleman. Also in Index.

CHAPTER 7. THIS I SHALL HAVE TO REVISE

CHAPTER 8. Last paragraph on page 115 Practice instead of practise.

CHAPTER 9. O.K.

CHAPTER 10. 1st paragraph Aleister instead of Aleistar PAGE 167.
2nd Paragraph Gance's Mater Dolorosa
4th paragraph should be "It opened at the Capitol Theatre, New
York."

CHAPTER 11. Page 189 Paragraph 2. " jeune premier of the twenties" (not
thirties)

CHAPTER 12. I must revise this chapter and bring it up to date

So all the chapters are O.K. with amendments except Chapters 7 and 12 which
I must revise.

There will not be a reprint of the English edition so if you follow
your plan of using English and Italian this will be the only version available in
English.

I have negatives and prints of all the illustrations. Do you want to
use them all or less or do you want new illustrations. I think my selection
for the book were the better ones. There is however one beautiful still from
BAROUD which I would like to use.

. I cannot get hold of the plates of the book. The publisher has disappeared
and can't be found.

I'll certainly give you all the help I can with proofs etc.

Liam O'Leary   29 June 1992

for
Alice Terry-Ingram

Rex Ingram, pageant-master

                 — *Finnegans Wake,* James Joyce

I am too proud to be a parasite
And if my nature wants the germ that grows
Towering to heaven like the mountain pine
Or like the oak sheltering multitudes
I stand not high it may be — but alone.

               — *Cyrano de Bergerac,* Rostand

No one but God and I knows what is in my heart.

              — *Song of the freed slaves.*

Contents

Foreword

This book attempts to tell the story of a famous and interesting film-maker during one of the most exciting and fruitful eras of the cinema. It is the result of years of intermittent research and detective work in which I was particularly lucky to have the help of people who knew and worked with Ingram. My starting point was an article by George Geltzer, a pioneer of research into American film history whose co-operation was most helpful.

The history of the cinema had been taken too much for granted, and until recently that of the American screen was the most neglected. There had been very little research from official sources — the industry itself, archives, academies, etc. The lone operator and enthusiast had often to work with little or no co-operation from those most in the position to help. Scattered throughout the world are individuals and organisations, each with a part of a jigsaw puzzle which has never been properly assembled. In some ways this creates an excitement and a sense of urgency, but a generation of knowledgeable people is now passing away. Apart from its ephemeral uses, the cinema has a legacy of great films and great artists. Their story is now fading.

For the film enthusiasts of this generation the prospect is better. There is an awareness of the need to record and assess the contemporary cinema scene. However, it was not until about 1935 that film archives began to conserve the heritage of the film, although the development of those archives was for many years hampered by lack of co-operation and finance. In Europe the delving into the past continued extensively in the official archives of each country, but scant attention was given to the detailed record of the American cinema, the most powerful and influential branch of the seventh art. It was left to the limited resources of two semi-private organisations to carry on the works of preservation as best they could — The Museum of Modern Art, New York and George Eastman House, Rochester N.Y. However, in the past few years the American Film Institute and other organisations are endeavouring to make up for far too much lost time and are systematically preserving the story of Hollywood.

I chose Ingram as a subject because of his importance as a distinguished film-maker of the twenties. There was, I must confess, another motive. Rex Ingram was an Irishman and Ireland's contribution to the cinema, for whatever reason, has been, in a specific sense, negligible. Officially Ireland had no continuous tradition of film-making, no film archive, no film school. Who else could we claim? — Herbert Brenon and, in the field of scientific film, Lucien Bull certainly. John Ford we can perhaps claim at second hand. But he is an Irish-American. And Robert Flaherty is closer to the German strain in his family than to the Irish. Perhaps I had a third motive. I clearly recall the great pleasures of my boyhood film-going which included seeing *The Four Horsemen of the Apocalypse* and *Scaramouche,* and *Under Crimson Skies.* This book, then, attempts to pay a debt.

Ingram was, above all, the great pictorialist and romantic of the cinema of the twenties. Nor was he without influence. As far away as Japan a very different type of director, Yasujiro Ozu, confessed to having been drawn to the cinema after seeing Ingram films. David Lean said in a recent interview: 'The man who really got me going was Rex Ingram. He directed *The Four Horsemen of the Apocalypse* and *Scaramouche*; he made Valentino a star, he made Novarro a star; and in everything he did the camera-work was impeccable.' Dore Schary could write many years after Ingram's death: 'The top creative people we think of in the early days of films are all directors — David Wark Griffith, Rex Ingram, Cecil de Mille, Erich von Stroheim.' Michael Powell said of him: 'A great man. The greatest stylist of his time, not excepting von Stroheim.' Harry Lachman put it this way: 'One of the greatest, a fine dramatic sense, a very fine pictorial sense and a perfectionist.' John Seitz, Ingram's cameraman for many years and the distinguished photographer of such films as *Double Indemnity* and *Sunset Boulevard,* thought him 'the most colourful and interesting character I ever met in my life', while L. H. Burel who has worked with almost every important French director of the past fifty years confessed: 'I have worked with many great directors, but the only one I can compare him with is my friend Robert Bresson.'

In attempting to tell Ingram's story I am under a debt to many people and these are credited in an appendix to this book. There are some, however, I would like to refer to here. I had the pleasure of meeting Lt-Colonel F. C. Hitchcock, MC, OBE, who went to the greatest pains to give me a picture of his brother's childhood and to help in every way he could. This has become all the more precious since his death some years ago. Ingram's early friends, Mrs Cherrie Gill, Major R. D. Greer and Dr Kenneth M. Greer have devoted much time to assisting me, while the contribution of John Seitz has been most enlightening. Jean Comte de Limur and Max de Vaucorbeil as well as Orlene, Comtesse Armand d'Aix shared their memories with me.

The valuable help of Mr George Geltzer and Mrs Eileen Bowser of the Museum of Modern Art, New York, in compiling the filmography cannot be overestimated. As to Alice Terry, I cannot express my gratitude enough for her help, interest and patience. My only hope is that this book will not be unworthy of the memory of her distinguished husband. To my friends at the George Eastman House Museum, Rochester, USA, Mr James Card and Mr George Pratt, I tender my grateful thanks. Mr Kevin Brownlow made available records of interviews, with von Stroheim and Grant Whytock and Mr James Ursini supplied me with an extensive interview with Mr John Seitz. These, I regard as major contributions to the book.

Liam O'Leary

1 Ireland

The following notice appeared in the births column of *The Irish Times* of 18 January 1893: 'HITCHCOCK, Jan. 15th at 58 Grosvenor Square, the wife of Francis R. Montgomery Hitchcock, of a son.' The boy's name was Reginald Ingram Montgomery Hitchcock, but he was to receive much wider publicity in later life as Rex Ingram, film director extraordinary, mentor of stars like Valentino, Novarro and Alice Terry. In the same newspaper that announced his entry into the world there were two other items: 'The Ultimatum to Morocco; Sultan consents to pay indemnity for the murder of Juan Trinidad and 'Mexican Joe's Wild West Show at the Rotunda'. The newly born babe was destined to have close ties with both Morocco and the Wild West.

His parents were married on 16 June 1891 at Zion Church, Rathgar, a fashionable quarter of Dublin. Kathleen Ingram, the daughter of the chief of the city fire brigade, was a gentle cultured girl interested in music and painting who had been educated in Ireland and on the Continent. Her husband, then studying divinity at Trinity College and son of a civil engineer of Dublin and London, had already distinguished himself as a classical scholar, having won the Berkeley Medal in 1889 and having taken his BA the year before his marriage. The couple went to live in Rathmines in a one-storey red-brick house, part of a housing scheme for officers from nearby Portobello Barracks. The year the first son was born, Francis Hitchcock took his M.A. degree and the following year he entered Holy Orders, being appointed Curate of St Mary's Parish on the north side of the city. This led to the family moving to the North Circular Road where on 15 March 1896 a second son, Francis Clere, was born.

Francis Hitchcock was a remarkable man who imbued his sons with his own deep love of learning and passion for boxing. Champion boxer of Trinity College, he was almost as proud of his boxing skills as of his scholarship. He was of a powerful physique and of a somewhat pugnacious character, tending to see people in terms of black and white, an attitude he transmitted to his children.

Major Roderick Greer recalls a visit by Hitchcock to his father, Canon Greer, as a guest preacher: 'As a very small boy I used to lie awake in bed in the night-nursery listening for Canon Hitchcock's footsteps, as it was his unfailing practice to come and talk to me before I went to sleep. On such occasions he would take pride in taking his jacket off, rolling up his sleeves and displaying to me his enormous biceps. Like his son who turned out to be a fine athlete, he was keen on all forms of sport.' Cissie Hitchcock, his sister, was the first woman to be accepted by the National University of Ireland at a time when Trinity College excluded women. Hitchcock senior's mother was a daughter of

Dr S. Ryan MD of Tipperary. His great-great-grandfather was the Chevalier de Johnstone, aide-de-camp of Bonnie Prince Charlie at Culloden and the author of *Memoirs of the Rebellion.*

The social background of the Hitchcock family was what today we would call the Ascendancy — the privileged class who represented Britain's interests in Ireland. To summarise briefly a long and complicated history, Ireland had been under British domination for seven hundred years but this was a domination which was consistently resisted throughout the ages. Irish chiefs and land-holders were driven from their territories and the estates were planted with English colonists. Very often the colonists succumbed to the charm of Ireland and very often led the national resistance against British claims, as did the Protestant Wolfe Tone in 1798, and Emmet and Parnell in later years. At the end of the last century the national cause was at a low ebb. The famine of 1847 had dealt a deadly blow, and the failure of the Parnell and Fenian movements had produced an apathy which was not to be broken until Pearse's rebellion of 1916. Families like the Hitchcocks, whose traditions were British, lived comfortable untroubled lives supporting the status quo. The subtle charm of Ireland had taken hold of them and absorbed them just as they had absorbed it. They might service the British Empire and supply the imperial armies, they might follow with interest the far-flung battle-line, but they were proud to live in Ireland and proud to be Irish. Yet they would regard any desire for freedom from British rule as mere foolishness. This caused a barrier between the mainly Protestant ascendancy and the Catholic majority of the Irish people. But Ireland is a land of ironies. Its nationalist leaders were often Protestants, and at the end of the last century it was the scholar Hyde, and the poet Yeats, two Protestants, who kindled the flame of national consciousness, that Ireland must be Irish and not West British. But while one can generalise about politics, in practice people live their lives not too troubled by theories. Scholarship and the arts leap barriers which the politician regards as insurmountable. So it was with the Hitchcocks, although the natural milieu of their lives was that of privileged comfort coloured by the glamour of military heroics.

Reginald, who was familiarly known as Rex, did not remain long in Dublin. His father was sent to Nenagh, Co Tipperary, as curate, where he remained from 1898 to 1901 when he went to Borrisokane (1901-3). The open-air country life appealed to Rex and his brother. Their father encouraged them in games and horsemanship, and they had their own animals to ride. The Reverend Mr Hitchcock settled down to his duties and became particularly friendly with the Catholic parish priest, Father Maher. There is a story that the two clergymen met on their way to their respective churches one Sunday morning and Father Maher asked the Reverend Hitchcock 'And what are you preaching about?' '1 Thessalonians 5,' replied Hitchcock. 'Ah, sure I'm talking to my crowd on how to improve their butter-making,' came the reply. One gathers that Father Maher was a 'character'. He left a deep impression on Rex who often accompanied him on his crow-shooting expeditions. Father Maher wore a tall silk hat for such occasions which he would give to Rex to hold while he raised his gun and let fly at the crows. In later life Rex often spoke about him and in an article written in 1927 for the London *Daily Express* said: 'I am a fatalist, because it keeps me from worrying and takes some of the

Right: *Ingram's birthplace at 58 Grosvenor Square, Rathmines, Dublin.*
Above: Ingram's mother *on left of picture* (left), *and* father and brother (right).

responsibility off my shoulders. I am superstitious, perhaps because I'm Irish. Anyway, good omens encourage me, and bad ones I can avert by crossing my fingers and spitting. This I learned at the age of six from the Parish Priest of Borrisokane, Co Tipperary. It has yet to fail me.'

The family next moved in 1903 to the village of Kinnitty which was to be Rex's home until his departure from Ireland seven years later. He was twelve and his brother Clere was nine. Their father was now Rector of Kinnitty, an attractive village in what used to be known as King's County and is today the County of Offaly. The nearest towns are Birr and Roscrea and it is sixty-four miles south-west of Dublin. The picturesque Slieve Bloom Mountains overlook the district. Castle Bernard was the dominating household and other mansions included Lettybrook, Glenview and Cadamstown House, most of · which suffered damage in the war-ravaged early 1920s. There were also many remains from Ireland's past. Kinnitty was once the site of the monastery of St Finian (557-839) which was destroyed by the Danes, but later restored. Its abbot, Colga McConaghan, who died in 871, was considered the most elegant poet and historian of his time. Nearby stood O'Carroll's Castle which featured in the wars of 1641, and not far away was an old Danish fort. William Bulfin, author of *Rambles in Eirinn* (1907), thought Kinnity the most beautifully situated village he had seen and remarked on the Irish revivalist activities he found there. Although the Reverend Mr Hitchcock was much interested in Irish history and in the topography of the area, it seems unlikely that the awakening national consciousness affected the life of the rectory very much.

In his book *Midland Septs and the Pale* (1908) Francis Hitchcock dwells on the more romantic aspects of Kinnitty. 'There is a cluster of thorn bushes on one of the private avenues of Kinnitty, which only a Saxon would pass with impunity after dark.' And again: 'The Irish were also in constant fear of an unpleasant Goblin called Pooka, Shakespeare's Puck, who has given his name to Poolaphouca in Wicklow, and to Bohernaphuca, an uncanny lane that strides at right angles to the truly magnificent mountain road that runs from Kinnitty to Roscrea with the picturesque hills of the Slieve Bloom on one hand and the verdant plains and hills of Ely O'Carroll on the other. The writer has ridden past the place at all hours but has never seen anything so far of the Pooka.'

Kinnitty was just the place to bring out the romanticism of the sensitive and imaginative boy. It was a happy life at the rectory. Francis Hitchcock helped his boys with their studies. There were parties and home theatricals which he encouraged. Scenes from Shakespeare figured prominently, and Rex would recite *Ode to a Mouse* by Burns and Sidney Carton's speech from the scaffold. Young Clere remembers waving a gory sword and uttering 'See how my sword bleeds for the poor King's death.'

Apart from this, Rex sketched and listened to his mother's performances on the piano. But above all there was sport. Goal posts had been erected in the rectory fields and in an old loft a punch-ball was installed. Then there were visits to neighbouring houses, all steeped in the traditions of British military history. Events like the African wars were of prime interest to the boys, and their heroes were the outstanding generals of these events. It was, it must be remembered, before the days of film stars.

Amongst the neighbours Rex used to visit were Mr and Mrs Jonathan Darby of Leap Castle, Roscrea. Once the stronghold of the O'Carrolls, the castle was destroyed by the IRA in 1921. Mrs Darby, who wrote under the name of Andrew Merry, was the author of a novel about the Great Famine called *The Hunger*. There was a room in the castle said to be haunted and apparently one of the walls was stained with blood. This took Rex's fancy until he learned that Mrs Darby had touched it up with red paint.

While he was at Borrisokane, his mother gave him a present of a pedigree Irish water spaniel, who became his constant companion. He used to bathe in the Brosna river and to dive with 'Towser' from the bank near Drumcullen Bridge. When 'Towser' died in 1916 Rex was in Hollywood and received the sad news from his brother Clere then fighting in the French trenches.

All his life Rex was attracted by army life. He would ride to Birr Barracks to meet and caricature his military friends — as his passion for sketching and cartoon work had already developed. There he watched the polo matches and played a lot of tennis. In later years Rex met some of these men when he had achieved world fame and success. But many were casualties of the Great War, part of Ireland's contribution to a war which was not hers.

In 1905, it was decided that he would go to St Columba's College on the outskirts of Rathfarnham, Co Dublin, for a formal education. This college has a delightful situation on an elevated position overlooking the whole sweep of Dublin Bay. On either side and behind it lie the hills and valleys of the Dublin mountains with the charming Kilmashogue Mountain to its left. Dublin city is not far away.

After an accident on the playing field, the warden, the Reverend Mr Parker, was replaced by a brother of Stephen Gwynn, the Irish writer, a man more sympathetic to Rex and who encouraged his artistic leanings. At school Rex was something of a lone wolf. Amongst his schoolfellows opinions were divided

The Rectory, Kinnitty.

about him. One student thought him 'a spoilt, irritating and tiresome boy'. Another remembered him: 'Hitchcock's generation was mostly killed in the first war but there are still a number like myself who have survived and would remember Hitchcock well, as he was always a personality, though we thought an unpleasant one. He was never much of a scholar.'

A third view was expressed as follows: 'He was then tall for his age and very slight in build. As I remember him he was always very pale in complexion with dark hair. I knew then he was an artist in his outlook and to put it mildly the rough and unthinking life of a public school was alien to his nature. We had many conversations regarding these matters and as I enjoyed the games etc, I realised he suffered a lot inside himself.'

Perhaps the clearest description of him at the time was by his close friend, Roderick Greer: 'He was of a most kindly disposition. He was a devoted godson to my mother and a staunch friend to anyone he took into friendship. He was sensitive, quick to take offence and something of a turbulent spirit. He was extremely good-looking with his dark raven hair and blue eyes and was graceful and lithe in his movements. He was one of the outstanding characters in my life and it was a grief to me when I heard of his death . . . Most people of his nature with a streak of genius suffer on occasion from deep depression, but I cannot recollect him ever being other than good-humoured. When he smiled his face was quite transformed.'

He was fond of drawing and even took postal lessons from a London organisation. An interesting observation by a schoolmate emphasises this: 'It was a time when women wore picture hats and Hitchcock specialised in drawing wondrous damsels with picture hats, an accomplishment we thought sissy.' One has only to recall the hats worn by Alice Terry in *The Four Horsemen* and *Mare Nostrum* to see the fruits of these labours.

In spite of the picture that arises of the lonely isolated aesthete, one has only to look at the school records to see how he shone in another field. In cricket he was a fast bowler and the smaller boys were afraid to stand up to him. In 1908 he won the open 100 yd in 11 1/5 seconds as well as the 220 yd open and did well in the high jump, the long jump and several hurdle events. In rugby he was a wing-three-quarter for the school 1st XV. He showed brilliance, speed and was a prolific try-scorer. He had his honour cap for three seasons.

But it is his boxing activities that make his legend in St Columba's. He could be aggressive. Also he never hesitated to champion the oppressed against the strong man and the bully. These acts did not always make him popular, especially with masters whose authority he flouted. One of his exploits was a fight with a boy called McIntyre who was 'as strong as a bulldog and reckoned to be too strong for Rex'. It took place in the school library at night. Kenneth Greer recalls the occasion: 'My twin brother saw the fight, but I was caught in the dormitory by Prefect Hinds Major while attempting to sneak out to see the fight. What I did see very soon through the curtains of my cubicle was a very pale Rex returning to the dormitory with his coat over his upturned shirt-sleeves completely unmarked. His opponent, who appeared at breakfast next morning, had two black and almost completely closed eyes and a great swollen nose which I fear was broken. He had received a terrible hiding and the fight had to be stopped.' The blood-stained chamois-leather gloves were later

Left: *The Understudy, A drawing of 1910.*
Right: *Rex as a schoolboy.*

presented to his friend Roderick Greer by Rex. All this was occasioned by a playing-field quarrel.

Apparently he did not confine his pugnacity to the boys. He challenged one of the masters, 'asked him to lay down his master's robes and go behind the gymnasium to decide which was the better man'. The offer was not accepted and led to firm handling by the warden. He also tackled the gymnastic master who was taking it out on his fifteen-year-old friend, Roderick Greer. Rex returned the punishment with interest.

Towards the end of his school days he earned official disapproval by wandering up and down the dormitory at night dressed in the house-master's gown and bowler hat and singing rude songs.

Such a thorn in the flesh of authority was bound to fall foul of his masters in the long run although he was not always in the wrong. Eventually Rex left under a cloud at Easter 1909. He celebrated his departure from St Columba's with an atrocious piece of doggerel:

> I am going back to father.
> Back to dear old dad.
> Although I made him sorry
> I now will make him glad.

He returned for one term when the storm had blown over to play for the rugger team. The school lost, and in disgust at his performance he is said to have confined his beautiful honours cap to the WC — though I have heard that it still exists.

While at school he won the Knox essay prize, a much coveted attainment, for essays based on Southey's *The Life of Nelson* and Joyce's *Place Names of Ireland*.

The death of his mother, while under operation at the Portobello Nursing Home, Dublin, on 8 October 1908, was for Rex a shattering event. He had obviously adored her, and her loss left an emptiness in his life. It was this which ultimately decided him to leave Ireland and seek his fortune abroad.

One friendship was made in characteristic circumstances. The young Osborne Burke, son of a Dublin businessman and a new boy at St Columba's, fell foul of the school bully. Inevitably the matter had to be settled by the gloves. Rex took Master Burke under his wing and gave him a highly concentrated course of boxing, which did not prevent him from losing, but at least helped him to put up a better show than he would otherwise have done and ensured that he did not receive any further molestation from other troublemakers. This led to a close friendship with the Burke family and particularly with Cherrie and Osborne's other sisters, who were very fond of him and felt he needed mothering. He was a constant visitor to their home at 1 Sunbury Gardens, Rathgar, Dublin.

They remembered him as an intense and impulsive young man. He would lapse into long silences during which he brooded on his personal problems and projects and then would suddenly jump to life and dance around with the girls. In speech he had a nasality of tone which was not quite that of the American variety. He had an obsession with the number nine. 'I'll give you nine kisses', he would say or 'I'll buy you nine hats'. He would be very proud to be seen in Grafton Street with Cherrie who was older and more sophisticated than he was. If they passed any of his schoolmates, he turned to Cherrie and said 'I wonder what they are thinking of me now'. Without illusions about the depth of his affection for her, she was nevertheless very fond of him.

At the time of his return home in disgrace from St Columba's, he came up to Dublin and visited Cherrie. He had heard that the warden of the school was in Belfast where he was accustomed to playing golf at a particular course. Borrowing his fare to Belfast from Cherrie (he was always meticulous about repaying his borrowings), he eventually collared the warden in the middle of his golf game and had it out with him there and then. The result was that he cleared his honour and the warden sent a message of apology to Rex's father. This certainly reveals strong determination.

He once persuaded Cherrie to get her chauffeur to drive out towards St Columba's. This was after he had left the school. As they reached the school gate — it was apparently during holiday time — he slipped into the building and returned with the punishments book tucked under his jacket. The book has never been seen from that day to this.

He and Cherrie had two things in common. They were enthusiastic collectors of cartoon and picture postcards of well-known actresses of the day. Rex kept up his cartoon work, much of which he sent to Cherrie. He also explored the commercial possibilities of his talent. He had drawings published in various magazines. On one occasion he failed to get Combridges of Grafton Street, Dublin, to take some of his work and he stalked out of the shop saying that some day they would pay as much for his autograph. At this time he displayed an interest in advertising, in which he did a postal course.

On his return to Kinnitty he studied under his father's tuition. He made tentative enquiries about emigrating to Canada, but later became interested in South America and began to learn Spanish. By now Francis Hitchcock had produced the following works: *Clement of Alexandria, Augustine's Treatise on the City of God, Christ and His Critics, The Mystery of the Cross, The Present Controversy on Prayer, A Fresh Study of the Fourth Gospel, Types of Celtic Life and Art* and *The Midland Septs and the Pale,* as well as several pastoral studies. Dr Hitchcock was appointed Donnellan Lecturer at Trinity College in 1910. His duties often took him away from home.

Rex did not lead an entirely isolated life between school and the rectory of Kinnitty. He, his father, mother and brother had spent holidays in the pleasant seaside town of Youghal where their lodgings overlooked the railway station. Rex took particular interest in watching the engines being turned on the revolving platform prior to their setting off again for Cork City. He and his brother visited the big international exhibition at Cork in 1902 where no doubt his first interests in the life of the Arab world and the mysterious East were aroused by the considerable exotic elements of the exhibition. In 1910 he visited the Isle of Man with his father and painted a little picture of Bradda Head. On another occasion he travelled on the curious mono-rail West Clare Railway. He was a constant visitor at neighbouring 'big houses' where the glories of the British Empire were not always the topic of conversation and where he met people whose interests were based on literature and the arts.

His cards, illustrated with cartoons, which he sent to his friend Cherrie Burke give some idea of his personality at the time: '19th May 1910. Kinnitty: Many thanks my dear Cherrie for your letter. I shall write later on. Am very busy at present so instead of the promised swank I had only room for the "understudy". But let me explain. As you know the far-famed factory girl by repute I suppose you won't have much difficulty in locating her. The under-study part is the smile and hair, you will notice the clothes and headgear, though swanks are of a bygone day. This pawn office explains this. It is both amusing and interesting to watch the laundry and factory hands in the "gods" trying to study the smile and style of some star-turn lady with the result depicted on the other side. The buildings in the distance are merely the clue, as Sherlock Holmes would say, to her profession, being meant for the factory chimneys. They are not part of picture, that is, not just across the road but a little inset as it were of her working field. Send me a Gibson if you have one. I've started a collection. Will write soon. Best love. Rex.'

He exchanged photos of the glamour girls of the day as well as drawings by Harrison Fisher and Charles Dana Gibson. He asked for news of Dublin friends and happenings — and about a production of *The Only Way* (the dramatisation of Dickens's *A Tale of Two Cities*), for instance. In return he regaled Cherrie with local gossip — how a lot of drunken cattle drovers were arrested at a fair, how he learned to ride a motorcycle, how he met a daughter of Carl Rosa, director of the famous opera company, who actually knew the fabulous Maud Allen. His postcards indicated his interest in local 'types and characters', an interest that was to be characteristic of him all his life, whether he lived in Hollywood, the French Riviera or on the fringes of the Sahara.

Such then were the contents of his communications from the rectory, where he was studying for his entry into Trinity College. This was his father's ambition, but Rex himself was planning to leave Ireland. Eventually his father realised his determination and sensed the feelings which were driving him away from familiar scenes which had now painful associations for him. He never reconciled himself to his mother's death.

The matter was decided as follows. Francis Hitchcock had a friend in New Haven, Connecticut, named Gordon Burt Hitchcock, who was no relation but who had become a friend through reading Dr Hitchcock's books. On hearing about Rex, the American Hitchcock replied that on no account should Rex be encouraged to go to South America, but that he himself would look after him and would be able to get him a job with the New Haven Railway Company. This was agreed and Rex was given his fare to the States by his father.

His brother Clere tells the story of the departure:

The afternoon before he left home — the rectory, Kinnitty, he and I went to say goodbye to Captain and Mrs Drought of Lettybrook, and had tea with them and their family. On our return home it rained heavily and we got awfully wet which was awkward as Rex was leaving early the next morning to catch a train at Roscrea for Queenstown and his boat, the *Celtic,* for the USA. At 6.30 am we left on a lovely morning from the rectory, Kinnitty, for Roscrea railway station across the Slieve Bloom Mountains by a road called Boharaphuca — the way of the spirits. As we climbed the road we always dismounted from the outside car as the

gradients were too steep for the horse. We could see the Shannon glisten-
ing in the morning sun and the Devil's Bit Mountain, also the great keep of
Leap Castle. I went with him to see him off at Roscrea as father was away
delivering lectures at Trinity College, Dublin.

And so I waved him farewell, not to see him again for twelve years
when he came to France and I stayed with him in Paris when on leave (he
was working on the preliminaries of *Mare Nostrum*). I returned home
very, very miserable, I remember, for he had always been such a kind
and gay brother to me, particularly since the death of our mother in 1908.

Rex later wrote his own version of the departure. He was not always a reliable
authority on his past. Either his memory was none too clear or he indulged in
fantastic improvisations for the benefit of journalists. Alternatively, facts were
distorted by the journalists themselves. Here is the story as told in an
unpublished manuscript:

In January I had turned sixteen. [In January of 1911 he was eighteen]
and my mind was made up: I was going to try my luck in the United
States. My father did not oppose me. He gave me my passage to New York
and some money and a letter to an American gentleman he had had some
correspondence with. I had an uncle in San Francisco, but my father said
it was too far away, and anyway he did not want to write to his brother as
they had not seen each other for years and he had an idea they were not
on speaking terms, although he was not sure if it was this brother or
another brother he was not on speaking terms with.

Then he said he would have Father Sullivan come up and make a list of
all the things I must avoid when I got to the States.

We went to see another friend and he said — 'So it's to America now
you're going, Oh Lord. Well me lad, all I can tell you is this: never travel
unarmed in foreign countries'. And with that he made me a present of. a
five-chambered revolver of the percussion-cap type.

My brother was very downhearted about my going, and he held my
hand all the way to Birr [Clere spoke of Roscrea] and cried a little now
and then. Of course, if my father had not been away in Dublin he
probably would not have felt so badly. My brother was the only one at
the train and he just clung to my arm and bit his lips to keep from crying.
Then the whistle blew and I hugged him and boarded the train — I leaned
out of the window and waved to him and he kissed his hand to me and I
saw him turn away as the train rounded the bend. He was leaning against
the wall of the signal box with his face buried in the crook of his arm, and
although I could not hear them, I could feel his sobs . . . and fifteen years
were to pass before we should meet again, and then in an hospital at
Davos Dorf in Switzerland. Three years in the Ypres salient had left him
with one lung, and at that he was lucky to have anything at all left of him
which is more than was left of most of the Leinster Regiments that had
gone to France.

At last I was on the tender headed out towards the bulk of the White
Star liner *Celtic*. Near me a girl, with grey eyes and a dark skin and her
hair tied in a silk scarf, was clinging to a man's arm. He kept talking to her

and coughing as well, and when we pulled alongside the *Celtic* she began to cry and hang onto him the way my brother had hung on to me, and it was her brother too.

And then the tender pulled away and people went to their cabins. I stayed on deck and leaned over the rail and began to think, and I realised how little thinking I had done for weeks — everything had been happening so quickly. I wondered how my brother was and how my father was, and here I was myself on the boat and not knowing a soul on it, and on the way to the United States where I did not know a soul either. As we steamed out of the harbour we passed the American flagship and the stars and stripes were waving from the stern and I took off my hat and then I heard a woman's cry and turned. It was the girl who had been on the tender with me. She was waving the scarf that had been around her hair and her hair had become undone and it blowing long and dark, and she cried again though no one could hear her: Goodbye . . . Goodbye . . .

And that was the last I saw of Ireland, with the girl standing there at the rail, and her hair blowing, and beyond her blowing the stars and stripes, and the grey Irish coast slipping away . . . slipping away, slowly — and for how many years!

Then a feeling of loneliness came over me, like it came over the girl and over my brother, and with it my courage left me, and left me too the spirit of adventure that had got me this far, and I wondered what was going to happen to me, and if I had not been a fool . . . and I walked away so that I could not see the Irish coast any more, because I was beginning to feel a tightening in my throat and I took my place by the forward starboard rail, and I looked out towards the open sea, and there was a white wall and white caps as far as the eye could see, and everything was grey and sad from this side too, only here there was menace as well: the heavy sea, waves breaking high over the bow, clouds scurrying, and as I looked, suddenly the sun broke through the clouds and three shafts of sunlight lit up the sea ahead.

There are some discrepancies in the two accounts. Rex seems to think he caught his train from Birr while Clere makes it Roscrea.

There is a record that Rex reached New York in the *Celtic* on 3 July 1911. He was never to see Ireland again.

On the 10th of the following August Rex's father married again. There is a romantic story of his sitting weeping all night on his first wife's grave to receive inspiration as to whether he should provide a new mother for his two boys. His new bride was the widow of an old colleague at Trinity College, Mrs Annie Isabel Trail, daughter of John Olphert Gage, a resident magistrate of Coleraine, Co Derry. The marriage took place in Coleraine. Apparently the two boys did not take kindly to their stepmother. By the time the marriage occurred Rex was in America and Clere was soon to enter the British army which he was to chronicle in his book *Stand To*.

2 The Apprentice

Rex Hitchcock was met in New York by his sponsor and namesake, with whom he was to live at New Haven, Masachusetts. Mr Hitchcock, who was connected with the New Haven railroad, would get Rex a job before he went to Yale to study sculpture. Rex always thought very highly of this kindness. Although being of an independent turn of mind, however, he more than likely did not make any demands on Mr Hitchcock, but made his own way as best he could, keeping his moments of difficulty to himself. Later descriptions of his life in the New Haven stockyards have been exaggerated into highly dramatic conflicts with characters who smack more of the Wild West than the East Coast. Rex may have been sensitive and introspective, but he was also arrogant and tough. No doubt his training as a boxer stood him in good stead.

The first record of his appearance at Yale reads as follows: 'Enrolled as a regular student, 2 Jan. 1912. Reginald I. Montgomery Hitchcock, King's County, Ireland. 16 Woolsey Street.' The New Haven address was probably his patron's home. The only other relevant entry in the Yale register is 'enrolled in the Sculpture Class 26 Sept. 1912. Reginald I. Montgomery Hitchcock. 16 Woolsey Street.'

In Yale his sculpture teacher, Lee Lawrie, a pupil of St Gaudens, formed a lifelong friendship with him. Lawrie was himself a sculptor of some distinction (he was later to design the Atlas statue outside Rockerfeller Centre) and took considerable interest in his pupil, whose work was more than promising. In 1950 he wrote to Rex's father on the occasion of Rex's death: 'Sometimes we hear someone spoken of as a "shining Light". Reginald, wherever he happened to be, whether in the class-room, in a gathering of people, or at work, radiated the fine elements of his personality. I believe he had more abilities and a finer grace in exercising those abilities than I have seen in anyone else I have ever known. His discerning judgement on the Fine Arts used to astonish me. Even when I first knew him he could see the best points in a work of art, and this same gift allowed him to see the good and the best in whatever came within his consideration. I miss his constant and warm friendship.'

Other friends at Yale included the painters Thomas Hart Benton and Harry Solon. At the office of the *Yale Record* one of his colleagues was Frank Tuttle, afterwards to make a name for himself as a film director in Hollywood. Rex was a frequent contributor to the *Yale Record* as a cartoonist, even after he left Yale for the movies. His style was somewhat reminiscent of the work of Phil May whom he admired. His drawings show a good sense of characterisation particularly of eccentric types, stage Irishmen and cowboys, but where they are used to put across funny stories they reveal a rather schoolboyish naïveté and a

Sketches on the back of an envelope while at Yale.

degree of 'undergraduate' humour.

Apparently he was in fairly constant contact with New York. He earned his way by taking up odd jobs of a varied kind in holiday time. He also undertook boxing engagements. There was at one time, talk of his going to sell motor-cars in Havana.

One always has to allow for his innate capacity to dramatise situations but he was adding to his knowledge of life in many and highly coloured ways. When his old friend, Cherrie Burke, arrived in New York with her father, he gave her picturesque accounts of his new life in the States. He was most anxious to take her to a dance at Yale but her father was loathe to trust his daughter to the care of this wild young man. However, Rex was not to be thwarted. He discovered that Mr Burke was interested in preparing an article on American affairs for a London newspaper and wished to penetrate the inner circle of the White House. He learnt that President Taft's secretary would be at Yale. He accordingly made an agreement with Mr Burke that if he were allowed to bring Cherrie to the dance he would arrange an interview between Mr Burke and the secretary, which he did.

At the dance he appeared dressed as a cowboy and caused some consternation by going up onto the balcony and firing shots through the window onto the square outside. He shouted 'I got him. I got him.' During the night he couldn't take his eyes off a blonde young woman who was present.

Another exploit was to make a model of the campus cop, one Jim Donnelly, which he sold to the students. He often posed for Lee Lawrie who was doing a series of sculptures of Civil War generals.

Rex made many friends at Yale. Margaret Harmon Graves remembered him: 'He seemed to have a wide span of vision, which, coupled with his sensitive mind, made him quite noticeable.

'He was unafraid, with a wonderful self-assurance, a complete confidence in his own ideas. They were usually original and his enthusiasm for them was tremendous. He had a powerful drive to his desire for accomplishment and always seemed busy, busy.

'Girls seemed to have no particular attraction for him.

'At Yale he seemed to us to be a gay, happily well-balanced young man with a sparkle to his personality which won friends and opened doors. In looks he appeared very slender, much as a youngster of seventeen or eighteen who had not yet acquired his full growth.

'Once in a while, while working in the studio, he would sit on a stool by my modelling stand and spend the whole afternoon regaling me with the wildest and most varied tales, all stories created on the spur of the moment. He seemed quite carried away with the pouring out of all his creative imaginings. It was fun listening to him.'

In 1913 his room-mate at New Haven, Horace Newsome, took him home for the holidays to Long Island, New York, where he was introduced to Charles Edison, son of the famous inventor and film industrialist. Naturally the conversation turned to films. It appears Rex had not thought much about them even though he must have seen them in Ireland. The friends went to see *A Tale of Two Cities* made by Vitagraph in 1911. This three-reel film of the Dickens novel was much in the style of its day, but had an intelligent script, was photographed beautifully and boasted Maurice Costello in the romantic role of Sidney Carton, while the minor role of the little seamstress on the scaffold was played by a newcomer, Norma Talmadge. In the leading roles of the lovers were Leo Delaney and the beautiful Florence Turner.

It is easy to see how this film appealed to young Hitchcock and it was to spark off an interest in the cinema which determined his future career. He knew the novel and the play and here it was in a new medium. The skill and craftsmanship of the Vitagraph films are rather under-estimated today — in contrast the films of the Biograph Company have gained undue importance because of their association with D. W. Griffith, key figure in the later history

Rex with Sally Crute, Richard Tucker and Mabel Trunnelle in THE SOUTHERNERS, *Edison 1914.*

of the cinema, while the work of the Vitagraph directors J. Stuart Blackton, William Humphrey, Maurice Costello, Robert Gaillard, Charles S. Gaiskell and Captain Harry Lambert is not given so much credit.

At this time, 1913, the film industry was centred upon New York. The Edison, Biograph, Kalem and Vitagraph studios were all in New York city; the New Jersey countryside was used for exteriors. Many studios developed in the latter area and it became an important film centre in its turn, particularly in the neighbourhood of Fort Lee. In 1910, D. W. Griffith took his players for a temporary sojourn to California and again in 1911 and 1912. But it was only in 1913 that the drift to Hollywood truly began, when it was found that the climate and the variety of scenery available were good for films.

The Edison Company had been one of the oldest American film companies. In 1883 Thomas Alva Edison, with the aid of his young British assistant, William Kennedy Laurie Dickson, had been searching for the moving picture image which would complement his discoveries in the realm of sound recording. At first the invention confined itself to the Kinetoscope, a peep-show machine using short bands of film which were sufficiently sensational at the time to attract viewers on a paying basis. The commercial exploitation of the Kinetoscope demanded more films and Edison was in business, founding a film studio called The Black Maria at Orange, New Jersey, on 1 February 1893. The subsequent development of cinema projection of images led to Edison extending the scope of his activities. He also attempted to control his patents and a trust war raged between the Edison adherents and the independent companies. In the end Edison lost his monopoly. In 1903 his star director, Edwin S. Porter, made the famous *Great Train Robbery* and other films of distinction. It was with Edison that D. W. Griffith began as a screen actor in 1907 in *Rescued from an Eagle's Nest,* which was made by another important director of Edison, J. Searle Dawley, who began as a scriptwriter and directed many hundreds of one-reelers and was later to become even more notable with *Famous Players.* Of the Edison players, Marc McDermott, Miriam Nesbitt and Mary Fuller were the best known.

At the time of Hitchcock's determination to make a career in films, the old Edison Studios were situated at 198th Street and Decatur Street in the Bronx. He took a job as general help advising on titling, details of sets, painting portraits of the stars. It was a time in film production when functions were not clearly defined. He also took a hand in scripting the stories and assisted in direction. One of his scripts was an adaptation of Charles Reade's novel *Hard Cash* directed by Hal Reid, the father of Wallace Reid, with Gertrude McCoy and Richard Tucker and released on 26 September 1913. This was a two-reel film, as was *A Tudor Princess* released on 26 December 1913 with Rex playing the Dauphin.

Rex was an extremely good-looking young man who photographed well and had much of the star-appeal of a matinee idol. He was not, however, a very good actor, and always gave an air of slight self-consciousness. Perhaps his critical intelligence was constantly functioning — not the best qualification for an actor, who must be capable of much more self-surrender. However, he was learning what made an actor tick; he saw mistakes being made by directors and saw how they could be corrected; he had the opportunity to become steeped

Rex Hitchcock, the Vitagraph actor.

in the whole atmosphere of film-making and be absorbed in the life around him.

He remained with Edison for something less than a year. Amongst the films in which he appeared were *The Necklace of Rameses* and *The Price of the Necklace,* both directed by Charles Brabin, a director whom Ingram admired. These were released in January 1914 and March 1914 respectively. In the former, Rex played the leader of a criminal gang. Then came *Witness to the Will* by George A. Lessey (January 1914), *The Borrowed Finery* (March 1914) and *The Southerners* (May 1914) based on a novel by Cyrus Townsend Brady. He also wrote scripts such as *The Family's Honour,* a story of the Spanish-American war released in 1914.

The Vitagraph Company of America was one of the interesting production companies in the early days of films. J. Stuart Blackton, a newspaper artist and Albert E. Smith, a professional magician, had been in the film business since 1896 and amongst other things had pioneered the cartoon film. In 1897 these two joined forces with William Rock to form the Vitagraph Company of America. The films produced in their Brooklyn studio were distinguished by a refinement and simplicity of presentation, although they often attempted quite elaborate subjects such as *Napoleon, Washington, Electra, The Life of Moses,* and particularly Larry Trimble's *Battle Hymn of the Republic.* They did not confine their films to the standard one-reel prevailing at the time, but often went to as many as three reels per subject. They had a fine roster of players: Maurice Costello, John Bunny, Florence Turner, Lilian Walker, Earle Williams, Norma Talmadge, Antonio Moreno, Helen Gardner, Leah Baird, Clara Kimball Young, William Humphrey, Mabel Normand and Julia Swayne Gordon. In 1925, the company was absorbed by Warner Brothers.

While with Edison, Rex introduced Jack Mulhall, the future star, to films, and the two moved to Vitagraph in mid-1914. There Rex became friendly with another charmer of Irish origin, Maurice Costello, then at the height of his fame.

Amongst the films Rex appeared in for Vitagraph were *Her Great Scoop* by Maurice Costello and Robert Gaillard, and *The Spirit and the Clay* in which he played a sculptor. This was directed by Captain Harry Lambert. Other films included *His Wedded Wife* by William Humphrey, *The Crime of Cain* by Theo Marston, *Eve's Daughter* by Wilfrid North, *The Artist's Madonna* with Lilian Walker, *The Circus and the Boy* by Tefft Johnson, *The Upper Hand* by William Humphrey, *Fine Feathers Make Fine Birds* by William Humphrey, *The Moonshine Maid and the Man* by Charles L. Gaiskell, *The Evil Men Do* by Costello and Gaillard, and *Goodbye Summer* by Van Dyke Brooks with Norma Talmadge and Antonio Moreno. He had a small role in *Beau Brummell.*

Here again he played a contrasting series of roles, from sympathetic hero to blackmailer. His fellow actors included Maurice Costello and his two daughters, Dolores and Helene, both to become big Hollywood stars, Leah Baird, Lilian Walker, Clara Kimball Young, and Naomi Childers, a member of a family closely connected with Irish politics.

Back in Ireland Rex's family received carefully censored reports of his adventures. The following letter to his aunt throws a light on Rex's personality and ambitions at this time in his career:

Top: *Rex in* THE SPIRIT AND THE CLAY, *Vitagraph 1914.*
Bottom: *The old Vitagraph Studio at Flatbush, Brooklyn, New York.*

Vitagraph Co. of America
E. 15th Street and Locust Avenue
Brooklyn N.Y.   March 17th 1915

My dear aunt Cissie: many thanks for the shamrock and your letter, which arrived today — The real thing is scarce over here.

I wrote to Aunt Edie and Uncle Ned — addressed them Lahore University — Lahore India — about a month ago.

You say something about selling out — Are you leaving Leinster Road? If you do sell your things at auction — which I hope you won't — because old furniture and old paintings have associations that make them priceless, let me know before the auction what the things are. I remember (I think I do) a four poster bed — a spinning wheel — and old bits of furniture and a wonderful picture over the drawing room mantel — don't sell that whatever you do.

If you are determined to, I'll start buying it by degrees! I am going — when I have made a pile or married one of the many heiresses here — a thing I hope I won't have to do as few of them are possessed of brains — I'm going to buy an old castle on the West Coast — I have a great number of talented friends — and I would like to start a place like William Morris where artists, sculptors, writers, designers, interior decorators could turn out really fine works with the commercial interest, while in good hands — being of second importance.

I would like that picture because over here everyone buys their ancestors, it is a relief to know that one has an ancestor attributed to a master who actually belongs to you. [This was probably the Chevalier de Johnstone who served with Bonnie Prince Charlie at Culloden. He was Rex's great-great-great-grandfather.]

I am working the finishing touches to another version of the *Rubaiyat of Omar Khayyam* — you know it — this is my first verse — I'll send you a copy when it is published. I'm going to illustrate it myself.

> Across the turrets from the clouds on high
>   A figure flashes with a joyous cry.
> The Herald of the Dawn is on his way
>   To drive the shadows from the morning sky!

> 'Awake' — his cry is like a trumpet blast
> 'Awake ye sleepers — it is morn at last!'
> I bow my head, Alas, another night
> With Haitim-Ti it seems I must have passed.

I am going to illustrate it in a rather unique way — illustrating the underlying thought, rather than the literal verse — here are a couple more:

> Of this sweet wine I want to drink so deep
> That rising from the soil where I shall sleep
> Its perfume [manuscript undecipherable]
> Will sway — and unperceived upon them creep

Rex with Clara Kimball Young in an early Vitagraph film.

Rex with Leah Baird in THE UPPER HAND, *Vitagraph 1914.*

Then I have some of the potter's shop —

> Leaning at dusk against the potter's door
> I watched him cast some clay upon the floor
> And thought — perchance it is my father's dust.
> Ah heedless potter that you thus ignore!
>
> Perchance the jar you turn upon the wheel
> Would say — could you or I its lips unseal
> My base is fashioned from a Sultan's head
> My head is fashioned from a beggar's heel!

So on — the end is

> Thou who hast drunk life's wine drink once again
> Only the final toast doth now remain
> Before those glazing eyes it stands — reach out
> The shrouded Vintner waits for thee to drain!

I have gotten some swords, Japanese prints, a Buddha — Chinese, and a drapery since I wrote you last. I'm getting some old Peruvian pottery soon — too — wait till I get that old castle. I'm going to have a room entirely Chinese — a room Gothic, a room Persian and one big junk shop — to use as a study and library.

Must end. Best love. Give Aunt Edie my love. I hope she got my letter before she called. Let me know about the picture when you write. Why don't you take a holiday to the U.S.A.?

Toujours

Rex

The obsession with *Omar Khayyam* was to continue for a long time. In a more moral tone his father had written: 'The sense of Society may be titillated with the poisonous perfume of the Rubaiyat but it is not permeated by it for there is always the virile optimism of Tennyson and Browning to act as an antiseptic in stirring the hearts and kindling the enthusiasm of our people.'

An interesting insight is given into Rex's way of life and background by Thomas Hart Benton, the distinguished American painter. They shared a studio together in a Bohemian and scruffy part of New York. In his book *An Artist in America* Benton relates:

I landed as if by instinct in the old Lincoln Square Arcade at 65th Street and Broadway.

That rambling building provided a refuge for everybody and everything. The doors of its long dark halls opened on every known sort of profession. Signs tacked on its walls told of Mme. So and So, astrologer from the court of Shah So and So, or of Dr. So and So, king of the muscle builders or of Madame Minnie who guaranteed Beauty and sure love through her treatments. There were dancing schools, gymnasiums, theosophical societies, theatrical agencies and all sorts of queer medical quackeries. There were prizefighters, dancers, models, commercial artists, painters, sculptors, bed bugs and cockroaches. Everything was in that building. Ambitious youth and the failures and disappointments of broken-down age jostled one another along its corridors. Settling in the Arcade I tried everything to make money, but without success, and frequently had to write home to my bitterly disappointed Dad for the wherewithal to eat. Finally here and there I did manage to pick up odd bits of work that I could do. I went around New York in French clothes and carried a cane. I met good fellows, went to parties and got in hot water with girls in whom I was much interested but with whom I could never get along for any satisfactory length of time. In the Arcade one of my young ladies in a fit of pique stuck a knife into me. Another tried to mix me up with the Revenue Officer for alleged hop smoking. Others were nicer. But with none could I get a permanent liaison . . . Through the influence of Rex Ingram who went from a novitiate in sculpture where I first knew him to the Movie Art, I got scenic jobs in the Fort Lee Studios and earned for a while the exalted sum of seven dollars a day. I looked up historical settings. I painted portraits of the movie queens of the day, Theda Bara, Clara Kimball Young, Violet Mersereau and others. I knew Warner Olin and Stuart Holmes. With the latter I had a great knock-down and drag out fight one night over a drunken party argument about who should entertain the ladies present on a player piano.

Rex Ingram who sponsored my movie jobs was in those days a highly temperamental young Irishman. He was full of theatrical romance and was always writing scenarios and trying them out on me. He used to get me in a corner, mess his hair up, roll his eyes and recite his concoctions in the most dramatic manner he could think of. I would sweat and take it for the seven dollars a day he controlled. One time Rex got it into his head that I might be made into an actor and gave me a part in a bar-room scene with Paddy Sullivan and Jimmy Kelly and a lot of other pugs of those days who put on fights for the movies. When that picture came out it went into theatres in Missouri and some friends of my father saw it, recognised me and told him about it. The old man was outraged and wrote me a scathing letter about where my artistic ambitions were leading me. Soon after, I quit my picture job over some quarrel about my pay.

While I was working in the movies, I never once regarded the material offered there as fit for serious painting. I missed the real human dramas that existed side by side with the acted ones and in my studio I painted the lifeless symbolist and cubist pictures changing my ways with ever whiff from Paris.

It was in this atmosphere Rex Hitchcock served his apprenticeship. While savouring this hotch-potch life he nevertheless pursued his new vocation passionately, working at the studios, making new contacts within the industry, observing the life about him and dreaming up his Gothic dramas which, within a year, he was to bring to the screen as a director in his own right.

Back in Dublin Mrs Greer, Rex's beloved godmother, took Rex's father to

Betty Nansen.

the Grafton Cinema to see their wandering boy in a Vitagraph drama. It was a sentimental occasion and both were moved to tears. By a coincidence the cinema orchestra was playing a composition by Mrs Greer's son Kenneth.

William Fox began his career in textiles, moving into the arcade and nickelodeon business and hence to film exhibition and distribution. In 1913 he was associated with the Box Office Attraction Company with Winfield Sheehan of Irish origin. At the beginning of 1915 he formed the Fox Film Corporation. He had sent his director J. Gordon Edwards on a trip to Europe to study the methods of film production in the course of which Edwards returned with the Danish star, Betty Nansen. In the meantime Frank Powell, another director, discovered another star, one Theodosia Goodman who became known as Theda Bara, the first great vamp of the screen. She was launched to fame and fortune in *A Fool There Was* directed by Powell, in 1915. Other important Fox stars of this year were William Farnum, Valeska Suratt, Nance O'Neill and Robert T. Mantell. Fox also engaged another Irishman, Herbert Brenon, who made film versions of *The Kreutzer Sonata* and *The Two Orphans*. Brenon embarked on a spectacular film in Jamaica with the swimming star Annette Kellerman — *Daughter of the Gods*. This film was the occasion of much litigation and the departure of Brenon from Fox. The Fox Company was, of course, to be a major element in American film production for many years, sponsoring the works of directors like John Ford and Frank Borzage and such popular stars as Charles Farrell and Janet Gaynor, as well as F. W. Murnan's superbly beautiful *Sunrise* (1927).

Motion Picture News of 29 May 1915 announced: 'The latest recruit to the ranks of the Directing Staff of the Wm. Fox Film Corporation is Rex Ingram formerly of the Vitagraph forces. Mr. Ingram will be associated with J. Gordon Edwards in the new Betty Nansen production on which work will be started immediately. The title selected for this Photoplay is *Mother Love* and the drama itself was conceived and written especially for Miss Nansen by Mr Ingram after he had made a long and painstaking study of the great actress and her methods. Miss Nansen is supported by a company of dramatic artists headed by Stuart Holmes and Arthur Hoops.

Betty Nansen had been engaged by Fox for a series of films. She did not remain long in America, however, but returned to her native Denmark where today a Copenhagen theatre carries her name.

It was at this stage that he changed his name to Rex Ingram, the name by which he was to be known to the end of his days. Ingram was his mother's name.

The title of *Mother Love* was finally changed to *Should a Mother Tell?* It was copyrighted on 30 June 1915 and the story is credited to J. Gordon Edwards, the director, while Ingram was responsible for the scenario.

Other scripts which Ingram did for the Fox Company include *Song of Hate* directed by Edwards and featuring Theda Bara, another Betty Nansen film *The Wonderful Adventure*, Nance O'Neill's *A Woman's Past,* and Robert Mantell's *The Blindness of Devotion*.

With these scenarios Ingram's period of apprenticeship came to an end. He

Opposite page: *Betty Nansen, the Danish actress.*

was now aiming at higher things and he set out to make for Fox a story entitled *Yellow and White* which told of a young white girl lured from Hong Kong to captivity in the home of a villainous Chinese in New York, from which she is eventually rescued by a young artist who makes her his wife. It was to be an atmospheric melodrama full of exotic types and realistic detail drawn from New York's Chinatown.

The production got under way but Ingram, who had very definite ideas of his own, soon clashed with the top executives in Fox. In the middle of shooting he realised that his future lay elsewhere and commenced negotiations with the up-and-coming Universal Film Manufacturing Company, under the benevolent despotism of Carl Laemmle. It was with this company that, as a fully-fledged director, he was to take the first steps up the ladder of success.

Theda Bara, the first vamp.

3 The Young Director

The Universal Film Manufacturing Company was the inspiration of Carl Laemmle, a Jewish emigrant from Germany, who had been a farmhand in Iowa and later manager of a clothing store in Oshkosh, Wisconsin. He opened a store in 906 Milwaukee Avenue Chicago on 24 February 1906 which in the evenings was turned into a cinema which ultimately became Laemmle's chief interest. Within six months the business prospered and he now ran a chain of cinemas as well as a film exchange. His film partner was a Robert Cochrane who interested him in films in the first instance.

The Motion Picture Patents Company, a trust which tried to monopolise the new industry, met one of its staunchest opponents in Laemmle, who, with his partner Cochrane, openly attacked the trust on 12 April 1909. Up to 9 April 1917 there was a constant battle, with defiance of injunctions and other legal disabilities imposed by the trust.

In 1909 Laemmle sent Tom Cochrane to New York to form a film production company — The Independent Motion Picture Company, better known as IMP. He used the facilities of the Actophone Studio at Eleventh Avenue and 53rd Street, New York. William V. Ranous of Vitagraph, a former fellow-actor of Ingram, became his director. The first film was *Hiawatha* with Gladys Hulette. The following year he added Florence Lawrence of Biograph, perhaps the first *known* film star, as well as Mary Pickford, whom he lured from Griffith at the then enormous salary of $175 a week. Mary's first film was directed by a young man named Thomas H. Ince of whom more would be heard. This was *Their First Misunderstanding* with Owen Moore, who had secretly married Miss Pickford. To escape the persecution of the trust a base was established in Cuba. Another of Imp's players was King Baggott, later to become an important director.

Persecution from the trust and dissensions amongst the rebel film-makers led to Laemmle and his associates forming the Universal Film Manufacturing Company on 8 June 1912. It was this company, in spite of the disapproval of Laemmle, which made the famous *Traffic in Souls,* directed by George Loane Tucker, premiered at Joe Weber's Theatre on 24 November 1913. At this time Universal had been making one-and two-reel films but this was six reels long and dealt with the white slave traffic. It showed large profits and attracted the comments of the regular dramatic critics for the first time in screen history. One of Laemmle's closest partners was Patrick Antony Powers of Waterford who had come up in the world from a smithy in Buffalo.

It was the company which gave Rex Ingram his first chance as a director. A fellow countryman of his, Herbert Brenon, was also employed by Universal.

Top: BROKEN FETTERS, *Universal 1916. Ingram with his Chinese players. Duke Hayward at camera.*
Bottom: THE GREAT PROBLEM, *Universal 1916. Kittens Reicherts, Dan Hanlon and Violet Mersereau*

Ingram was thoroughly familiar with all phases of production by this time, and his cultured background gave him an advantage over the rag-tag and bobtail who found their way into movies. Moreover he did not underestimate his own capabilities, so it was with considerable self-assurance that, at the age of twenty-three, he set out to film one of his own stories. Original negotiations had been for the film he was prevented from making at Fox, but his first film for Universal was his own story — *The Great Problem,* which dealt with the rehabilitation of the daughter of a criminal who falls in love with her benefactor and whose life she saves.

The reviews indicated that the social theme was rather unconvincing and that the film owed much to the vivacious personality of the young Violet Mersereau, who played a dual role of mother and daughter. The *Moving Picture World* admired the underworld scenes, the settings in general and the acting, although it complained of too many close-ups. The English *The Cinema* noted its bright entertainment with 'realism just sufficiently touched up to make it artistic and laughable'. It praised the lively performance of Miss Mersereau. Kittens Reichert in a juvenile role, Dan Hanlon as the criminal, Lionel Adams as the attorney, William J. Dyer as a crook and Howard Crampton as the

BROKEN FETTERS, *Universal 1916. Violet Mersereau and Charles Francis.*

THE CHALICE OF SORROW, *Universal 1916. Wedgewood Nowell and Cleo Madison.*

pompous butler were the principal players. The film was released in the USA on 17 April 1916 and was five reels in length. In England its title was changed to *Truth,* and it was distributed under the Universal-Bluebird banner. According to Ingram it cost less than $8,000.

Ingram now returned to his Chinese story, which had led to his leaving Fox. It was released in the USA under its new title, *Broken Fetters* on 3 July 1916 in five reels. Its scenes in Hong Kong and New York's Chinatown gave Ingram every chance to indulge his flair for the exotic and the delineation of strange characters. Again Violet Mersereau, Kittens Reichert and William J. Dyer appeared and the cast included the well-known Paul Panzer. The *Moving Picture World* thought highly of its production, acting and use of types, describing it as suspenseful, beautifully photographed and costumed.

The photography was begun on this film by Stanley Sinclair, but Ingram, who was most demanding and had definite ideas about how a scene should look

BLACK ORCHIDS, *Universal 1916*. Above: *Cleo Madison*, right: *Cleo Madison and Francis McDonald.*

on the screen, became dissatisfied and replaced him by B. C. ('Duke') Hayward, who was to work on many of his films. Ingram liked close co-operation with his cameraman. Born in London in 1880, and educated there, Hayward emigrated to the USA. A photographer for twenty years with Hearst Newspapers, he also worked with the Reliance-Majestic, Lubin and Universal Film Companies. Little is known of him after 1917.

Cleo Madison was a talented and intelligent actress who joined Universal about the same time as Ingram. He was a great admirer of hers and considered that she was the most natural actress with whom he had ever worked. For his next two films he provided her with two striking roles — as a mystical *femme fatale* and in a role based on Sardou's *La Tosca*.

At this time it was decided by Laemmle that the work of the Universal Company should be transferred from the Fort Lee Studios, New Jersey, to Hollywood, where Universal City was being established. So Ingram set off for

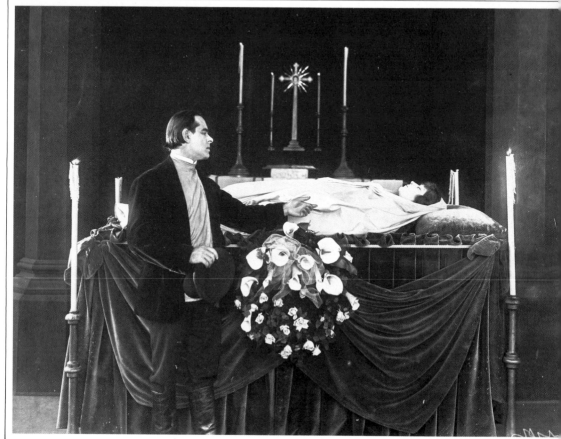

Top: THE REWARD OF THE FAITHLESS, *Universal 1917*. Left: *William J. Dyer;* Right: *Nicholas Dunaew in the tavern.*
Bottom: THE PULSE OF LIFE, *Universal 1917. Gypsy Harte.*

Opposite: THE REWARD OF THE FAITHLESS, *Universal 1917*. Top: *William J. Dyer and Betty Schade.* Bottom: *Nicholas Dunaew and Claire du Brey.*

the west coast where his future success lay.

The Chalice of Sorrow was *La Tosca* in a Mexican setting. It is the story of a woman who surrenders herself to a tyrant, or pretends to, in order to save her lover's life. It had a tragic ending. Ingram never hesitated to kill off his characters if he felt the story demanded it, and his next two films were to be unrelieved by any concessions to box-office preferences. Again the settings and acting drew praise from the critics, who appreciated the fine performance of Cleo Madison. The heavy was played by Wedgewood Nowell who was to appear in many Ingram films. This actor was born in Portsmouth, New Hampshire, and was educated at the University of Pennsylvania. He was a versatile artist having been actor, producer, pianist and violinist. His films included *The Corsican Brothers*, *A Man's Fight*, *Adéle*, *The Cheater* and *The Lord Loves the Irish*. *The Chalice of Sorrow* was released in the USA on 9 October 1916 in five reels. In England it was known as *The Fatal Promise*. Again the photography was by Hayward.

Black Orchids came next on the list. A favourite subject of Ingram, he remade it in the twenties under the title *Trifling Women*. This was a Gothic tale *par excellence* with castles, dungeons, noblemen, duels, poisons, erotic passions and the occult. The story was treated as a cautionary tale and set between a prologue and epilogue. Cleo Madison as the evil mystic Zoraide, Francis McDonald, Wedgewood Nowell and Howard Crampton as her victims, and John George, the little hunchbacked actor making his first appearance in an Ingram film, provided a strong cast. It even had a leading role for the famous Hollywood chimpanzee, Joe Martin. This highly coloured melodrama was the sensation of the year and was marked by characteristic Ingram production qualities of atmospheric settings and skilful direction of the actors. Its brutal aspects were too much for some critics and the morbid association of Zoraide and the chimpanzee was the subject of strong disapproval from some reviewers. The film was reminiscent of a Theda Bara movie. It was released on 1 January 1917 in five reels.

Hitherto the stories Ingram used at Universal had been his own. For his next two subjects, Ingram prepared the scripts from work by E. Magnus Ingleton. They were equally colourful and added Russia and Italy to Ingram's geographic range.

The Reward of the Faithless (known in England as *The Ruling Passion*) was released on 12 February 1917 in five reels. Originally Cleo Madison was to play the lead, but she quarrelled with Ingram and walked off the set. Her less experienced replacement, Claire du Brey, became a close friend of Ingram and his wife Alice Terry. The Russian Nicholas Dunaew, an old Vitagraph player, acted the poet who befriended the Russian noblewoman, shamefully exploited by an adventurer and his mistress.

None of the early films of Ingram is available now, even in the national film archives. But, by one of those rare strokes of luck, the first reel of *Reward of the Faithless* surfaced in a Dublin junk-shop when I was researching for this work. In this fragment of the film three locations are used — a household of a prince, a slum dwelling and a tavern. The first is elegantly furnished, the second is grim and realistically sordid and in the tavern scene strange types abound, including dwarfs and hunchbacks, ancient bearded faces, and the handsome impressive face of Dunaew as the hero. There is also a flashback scene in which the tale of a ring is told, how a poisoner steals it from the finger of a czar sleeping on his throne. The scenes in the slum immediately remind one of von Stroheim, who praised Ingram for his realism and who himself directed similar scenes in *Greed*. Indeed, shot after shot in the earlier film looks as if it might be from *Greed* which came seven years later. Significantly, Ingram was the only one von Stroheim would trust with the second cutting of *Greed*. The use of close-ups of natural types in the tavern scene are reminiscent of Eisenstein. There is also an effective rhythm used in the cutting of these scenes.

The film won praise from one British critic of *The Kinematograph and Lantern Weekly* for its production and photography, although the story was regarded as a mere series of sordid incidents, and the act of betrayal particularly unpleasant. The opening was attacked for its vivid depiction of an underworld inhabited by dwarfs, cripples, drunkards and degenerates.

Deformity amounts to an obsession in Ingram's work. Whether he used it as a superficial contrast to his handsome heroes and heroines, or whether it had a deeper motivation, it is hard to say. Another director who concentrated on human deformity was Tod Browning, whose scriptwriter, Willis Goldbeck, wrote *Freaks*. Goldbeck was a discovery of Ingram.

An extraordinary actor, John George, began his career with Ingram in *Reward of the Faithless*. This deformed young man was originally called Tufei Fatella and came from Syria. In 1911 he left his native country and by devious means arrived in the United States in search of his mother and sisters, who had previously settled in Nashville, Tennessee. In due course he ended up at the Hollywood casting bureau. He appeared with Lon Chaney in *The Unknown* and became a characteristic feature in Ingram films.

Nicholas Dunaew, the leading man for two of Ingram's films at this time is interesting as an example of the foreign talents that Hollywood was beginning to attract. He was born in Moscow on the 26th May 1884. His father was a nobleman and his mother Fedosia Bagrova came from a St Petersburg literary family. He was educated in Moscow and St Petersburg obtaining a degree in literature and also studied law. His debut as Franz Moor in Schiller's *Die Rauber* took place in January 1904 after which he toured Europe with his own company in plays by Ibsen and Tolstoy as well as his own plays *The Spider, The Vampire, The Terrible God* and *Two Nationalities*. Coming to America he played in Daly's Theatre New York, and in Jacob Adler's Theatre on the East Side in Tolstoy, Gorki, Ibsen and Andreyev. His entry into films came when Blanche Walsh engaged him to assist with decors and details of her production of *Resurrection*. He then became an actor with the Vitagraph company where he probably met Ingram. With Tolstoy's permission he prepared scripts of *The Powers of Darkness* and *War and Peace* which apparently were never used. Some of his appearances were in *My Official Wife, Call of the Past* and *The Winksome Widow*. He was equally successful in tragedy and comedy. In the twenties he had disappeared from the film scene but did act as advisor on Victor Schertzinger's *Siberia* (1926). As an actor he had a striking presence and looks most impressive in *Reward of the Faithless*. His performance is characterised by intelligent restraint. He also appeared in Ingram's next two films.

Overleaf: THE FLOWER OF DOOM, *Universal 1917. Yvette Mitchell and Frank Tokonaga.*

Ingleton's second story to be filmed by Ingram was *The Pulse of Life*, released on 9 April 1917 in five reels. This story of the luring of an innocent Italian girl to New York by an unscrupulous painter seemed to be a variation on the theme of *Broken Fetters* and did not commend itself to the critics. However, once more Ingram's direction was praised and the beauty of the sea scenes noted. Gypsy Harte played the girl, Nicholas Dunaew her brother and Wedgewood Nowell the villain. These three, along with Yvonne Mitchell, took the leading parts in his next film.

With *The Flower of Doom* Ingram returned to a Chinese theme. This was a complex, sordid story of gang warfare in Chinatown, in which the destinies of many people are woven together with an almost mystical doom shadowing the action. For Ingram it was another opportunity to create the atmosphere of a sinister underworld and the critics once more praised his direction and choice of locations. The characterisations also seem to have been excellent. It was the last film in which Ingram used Hayward as cameraman and nothing is known of the latter's subsequent career. The locations bring to mind the underworlds of Pabst's films and the mood and atmosphere of Delluc's *Fievre*. It was released on 16 April 1917 in five reels.

In *The Little Terror* he returned to light comedy, using once more his first star, Violet Mersereau, who had now appeared in three of his films. Miss Mersereau had been born in New York in 1894. She played *ingenue* roles on the stage before her great success in the Universal productions of *The Angel in the Attic* and *Little Miss Nobody*. She was to play opposite Jacques Gretillat in J. Gordon Edwards' spectacular production of *Nero* in 1922.

This was a story of the circus, of a wildcat girl rebelling against attempts to make her conform to society. It had a happy ending and was from a story by Ingram. Again Violet Mersereau played a dual role of mother and daughter, Sidney Mason acted the hero and Ned Finlay the disapproving grandfather. The critics found it entertaining, even though the characters were overdrawn and the plot slight. It was very much a Violet Mersereau vehicle. It was released on 30 July 1917 in five reels.

At this time Ingram was still very young, ambitious and impetuous. He had a lively intelligence and did not suffer fools gladly. His fiery Celtic temperament brought him into constant conflict with administration and he was not an easy director to get along with. He was a very loyal friend to those who were loyal to him, but he was quick to take offence and unforgiving once a breach had occurred.

His ideas were often ahead of his company's and his ambitious handling of *Black Orchids*, for example, made it run $2,000 over the estimate, a horrible extravagance in those days. Ingram himself was earning the princely sum of $300 a week at the time.

He had now directed eight films. From these he had gained considerable knowledge of his craft. Contemporary reviews constantly refer to his evocation of mood and atmosphere, fine pictorial qualities and the good performances he extracted from his players. These were to remain permanent Ingram characteristics. In the absence of the films, with the exception of the revealing fragment of *Reward of the Faithless*, it is difficult to assess precisely how they would stand up to present-day examination. Only time will prove if copies still survive. A fire at the Fort Lee studio where the negatives were stored may have sealed their fate. In the twenties, Universal sold off many of their negatives to other companies and individuals. Time has not been kind to older films and much early material has been lost through the indifference of the film industry to its products once they had served the immediate end of making money at the box-office. But contemporary reviews suggest that at this time Ingram had individuality and style and was in many ways an unconventional director.

But conflict with his patrons had broken out and in 1917 he was fired by Mr Sellers, his producer. Legend had it that he was sacked by Carl Laemmle because he had put every hunchback and dwarf in Hollywood on Universal's payroll. But it seems that the real reason was his openly expressed dissatisfaction with the way production was being managed. It was not the last time his frankness was to make him enemies. When he left he had still seven months of his contract to serve.

Below: THE FLOWER OF DOOM, *Universal 1917. Gypsy Harte and Gordon Keene.*
Overleaf: HUMDRUM BROWN, *Hodkinson-Paralta 1918. Ingram with Henry B. Walthall, Mary Charleson and Howard Crampton.*

4 Strange Interlude

On leaving Universal, Ingram was engaged by Paralta — W. W. Hodkinson Corporation to make two films with Henry B. Walthall — an actor of considerable stature whose 'little colonel' in *Birth of a Nation* brought him well-earned fame and who had since increased his reputation with a series of dramatic roles.

The first of these films was *His Robe of Honour*, released in seven reels on 15 January 1918. In the role of a shady lawyer, Walthall dominated a complex plot of intrigue and regeneration giving quite a good performance. As usual, the settings were outstanding and visual similes paralleled the actions of humans and animals. The leading female roles were taken by Mary Charleson, Walthall's wife, and Lois Wilson who later achieved fame as the heroine of *The Covered Wagon*.

On 15 March 1918 *Humdrum Brown,* another Walthall-Charleson film, was released. This was yet another rather trite version of 'local boy makes good'. Neither film can be regarded as a progressive step in Ingram's career. It was not a particularly happy period for him. A dip in his creative activities was paralleled by a troubled domestic situation. On 15 March 1917 he had married Doris Pawn at Santa Ana, California. They had been introduced by Cleo Madison. Doris was, at the time, appearing in serials and dramas with Universal. Rex's junior by three years, she was born in Norfolk, Nebraska on 29 February 1896 into a comfortably well-off family. Her father, Martin Pawn, was born in Berlin and her mother was also of German stock. At school Doris showed an interest in acting. She joined a stock company and at the age of seventeen visited California with her mother. The visit was to have lasted only three months but she obtained some small roles with Universal and eventually played in the famous serial *Trey O'Hearts.* She then joined Fox where she played in *Blue Blood and Red* for Raoul Walsh. In this year (1916) she had an accident and had to return home. After convalescence, she played once more for Universal and later joined Goldwyn to appear in *Toby's Bow* with Tom Moore, in *The Strange Boarder* with Will Rogers and in some fifteen films between 1921 and 1923 before she disappeared from the Hollywood scene in the mid-twenties. Blonde and blue-eyed, she was by all accounts a vivacious personality. She played a good game of golf and devoted herself to outdoor activities. At home she had conventional tastes in decor, but admired Omar Khayyam, whose poetry she kept constantly beside her.

But within little more than a year incompatibility of temperament led them to separate. They were formally divorced at the end of 1920 when Ingram was making his great bid for fame with *The Four Horsemen of the Apocalypse.*

Above: HIS ROBE OF HONOUR, *Hodkinson-Paralta 1918. Lois Wilson and Henry B. Walthall.*
Opposite page: *Elizabeth Waggoner, friend and benefactor* (top left); *Ingram as an officer of the Royal Canadian Flying Corps in 1918* (top right); *Doris Pawn, Ingram's first wife* (bottom).

In 1918 came a break with films. Ingram applied to join the US Signal Corps Aviation Section, but was turned down since he had only his first citizenship papers and only full citizens could be pilots. He then tried the Royal Canadian Flying Corps. Their records show that his period with them was from 9 October 1918 until he was discharged on 19 December 1918 and that he was granted an honorary commission as second lieutenant with effect from 1 January 1919. Various reports say that he was a flying instructor and was seriously injured in a crash when the metal of a propeller entered his lung. The army authorities have no record of any such crash but apparently this led to periodic illnesses during his life. He never saw any active service as the war terminated in November 1918.

Ingram's return from Canada was a very unhappy experience. He had left the Royal Flying Corps a very ill man and almost penniless. His pride did not allow him to let his family in Ireland know about his difficulties, but he was not

An Ingram illustration for Omar Khayyam.

entirely without friends. During this time, Elizabeth Waggoner, an art teacher in the Hollywood High School helped him greatly. He stayed with her for three months. Ten years after his death she wrote: 'I was in touch with Rex Ingram for all of thirty years of his colorful life — from the hour of our first meeting to the last week of his life on earth. A brilliant mind, a fine classical education and heritage, a fascinating personality. I would that you had known him! No one who did would ever forget him.'

Others who tried to help him were Bessie and Jesse Lasky. He got a job as a set director at the Lasky Studios but had to resign through illness. William and Anna de Mille were also friends at this sad time. One day Rex met Allan Holubar who took him out to the Universal Studios. At the time Holubar was directing Rudolph Valentino. Grant Whytock, who was working with Holubar on *Talk of the Town*, mentioned Valentino to Ingram, and Ingram made a screen-test of him. This indicates that he had Valentino earmarked before June Mathis started to promote him.

In 1954 I had the privilege of interviewing Erich von Stroheim, who told of his meeting with Rex at this time:

He was a very proud man and wouldn't have done the things I did. He never stooped, he never gave any publicity and was a little huffy — he was very Irish. And when a journalist made a slighting remark he resented it and refused to talk further . . . Our friendship came about in a funny way. Rex Ingram was a director at Universal when war broke out — the First World War. I only came to Universal near the end of the war, that is in about May or April 1918. I then didn't know Rex Ingram. In about January or February 1919 I was directing a scene in *The Devil's Passkey*, the second picture I made, and there was a man standing on the side in a khaki overcoat, an officer's overcoat, no hat and really good-looking. I mean good-looking isn't the word, he looked like a Greek god. And he looked rather provokingly at me, challengingly, kept his eyes without blinking, looking at me and it made me nervous. I didn't know who the hell he was and my position was a very cool one, people thought I was a German, and of course you can imagine that the people who had just lost some dear relatives in Flanders or somewhere else didn't like me very much. Aside from that, I had appeared in Austrian uniform in my first picture *Blind Husbands,* which didn't help to promote love and goodwill. So on seeing this khaki officer's coat I thought it was a man who had come back from the trenches who just wondered what I was doing here. Well I called my assistant Eddy Sowders and said 'Who is this guy?' He said, 'That's Rex Ingram.' I said, 'Who's Rex Ingram?' He said, 'That used to be the whitehaired boy here, a great director.' And I said 'What does he want?' He said, 'I don't know but I'll go and ask him.' 'So he went over, and Ingram said, 'What is this son of a bitch doing here? He's got my job.' He had been a director before the war and he went to fight for his country and when he came back there was no job for him — they told him, 'Sorry, but sorry it's filled.' So there it was. I had filled one vacancy — his. So he didn't like me very much, which was understandable. I went over and introduced myself — not clicking my heels as usual, but kind of friendly so that I wouldn't be too pompous. And we started talking and he said, 'Well you know it's very difficult for a man who comes back. I was a director here and now I'm through the war. I've been in the airforce and I have no money and I've no civilian clothes, it's kind of tough to see the ex-enemy having, so to say, my job.' I said, 'Well now, look, I mean I didn't take your job, I didn't know you, and what the company does — and I do believe the company did wrong in not giving you a job aside from mine. I mean I had nothing to do with it.' Well we got talking and then I, of course, had a bottle of some whiskey, Scotch, and I offered him a drink and we had two, we had three, and at the end after about ten or twelve we were very palsy-walsy. And then he proved himself a great friend in many ways; he even gave me a pair of boots that didn't quite fit his big feet and which I wore going into Death Valley, trench boots.

UNDER CRIMSON SKIES, *Universal 1919. Beatrice Dominguez, Noble Johnson and Elmo Lincoln.*

UNDER CRIMSON SKIES, *Universal 1919. The beachcombers.*

However, due to the good offices of Holubar and P. A. Powers, the influential co-founder of Universal who came from County Waterford, Ingram was invited to direct two films. The first of these to be released (actually the second film shot) was *The Day She Paid* based on a short story by Fanny Hurst entitled *Oats for the Woman*. The action was set in a high-class dress-designing establishment and had a theme reminiscent of *Lady Windermere's Fan*. A woman sacrifices her own reputation to save that of her stepdaughter. The settings and acting were much praised and the mannequin parades gave an opportunity for spectacular display. Francelia Billington, who had been von Stroheim's leading lady in *Blind Husbands*, played the lead opposite Charles Clary as the husband, while Harry van Meter was a villain. Alice Taaffe's small part in this film was to be her first step to stardom and to marriage with Rex Ingram. Typical subtleties of treatment included the use of hard lighting for the husband and soft lighting for the wife. Critics liked the film and it was clear that Ingram had made a significant come-back. The film was released in five reels on 5 January 1920.

A more important film however was *Under Crimson Skies,* released in six reels on 5 July 1920. It was an adventure story about gun-running in a South American republic and had many elements which appealed to Ingram. It was full of colour and excitement and featured the grotesque human characters which Ingram was so fond of introducing into his films. The central character of the adventurous sea captain was played by Elmo Lincoln, already famous as the first Tarzan of the screen. Noble Johnson played the black adventurer, Baltimore Bucko, while the feminine leads were taken by Mabel Ballin and Beatrice Dominguez, who later became Valentino's tango partner. One British critic took exception to its American jingoism but the film was popular, both in the States and abroad, particularly in France. The cameraman was Phil Rosen (later a director himself). Grant Whytock was probably involved in the editing of this film.

In addition to acquiring practical experience, Ingram was well aware of other developments in the cinema and certainly was familiar with the work of Griffith, George D. Baker and Maurice Tourneur, from whom he derived much inspiration. All these men had a highly developed pictorial sense. Griffith referred to Rex as 'one of my boys', though Ingram never worked directly with him.

In *The First Hundred Noted Men and Women of the Screen* (1920), there is a significant entry for Ingram: 'As a screen director he is looked upon as one of the men of the future. His sense of proportion is keen, his mind well balanced and the results of his artistic instincts stand forth in everything he does.' He was now building a considerable reputation. His salary at Universal was $300 a week. It seemed that his luck was turning.

At this time Rex lived in the old Hollywood Hotel which was quite an institution, where directors and film people could meet and discuss their ideas and ambitions. There he met Frank Brockliss who owned the rights of some stories which Rex wished to film. For some reason Brockliss was not in a position to accede to Rex's request but suggested he contact Richard Rowland, then manager of the Metro Studios. Rex had a backer if he could find a good story, and these would have served his purpose. Rowland said he had no

THE DAY SHE PAID, *Universal 1919. Francelia Billington. Alice Terry third from left.*

objection if Ingram could get Maxwell Karger, publicity man for Metro, to agree. Karger proved difficult. It was finally agreed however that Rex should direct for Metro, at $600 a week, the well-known American drama by James Herne entitled *Shore Acres.* The stories which Rex had wanted to do were by Jack London. However this first film for Metro proved to be a new beginning and the start of a period of fame and success for Rex.

Ingram directing THE FOUR HORSEMEN OF THE APOCALYPSE *on the studio lot.*

5 Miracle at Metro

As Ingram was to spend the greater part of his creative life with the Metro Picture Corporation, it is appropriate to outline here the story of its foundation and development. Al Lichtman, who had worked with Adolf Zukor, conceived the idea of getting Film Exchanges (the distributing machinery of the time) to put up money for film production which would be carried out by small organisations. To this end the Alco Film Corporation was formed in 1914 and one of its first offerings was *Tillie's Punctured Romance*, featuring Marie Dressler, Mabel Normand and Charlie Chaplin. The company only survived a few months, but late in January 1915 at the Hotel Claridge, New York, the shareholders decided to continue as the Metro Pictures Corporation. Richard Rowland, an Exchange man from Pittsburg, was chosen as president. Louis B. Mayer, an Exchange man from Boston, was to be secretary, Joe Engel, a New York agent, became treasurer and the counsel was J. Robert Rubin.

A considerable number of producers, who had worked through Alco, now affiliated with Metro. Their studios were scattered, but eventually J. Searle Dawley's studio at 61st Street and Broadway was to be the eastern studio of the Metro organisation. Amongst the stars engaged were Olga Petrova, Florence Reed, William Faversham, Francis X. Bushman, Marguerite Snow and Ethel Barrymore.

The first Metro release was *Satan Sanderson* in May 1915, followed by *The Heart of a Painted Woman, Shadows of a Great City, The Song of a Wage Slave* and *Barbara Frietchie*, the latter featuring the popular Mary Miles Minter. Louis B. Mayer left Metro in 1918 to promote the films of Anita Stewart. He was later to make a dramatic entry on the scene and to play a large part in Ingram's career. Rowland carried on with Maxwell Karger, a one-time violinist of the Metropolitan Opera, as production chief. A series of cheap programmes each costing no more than $20,000 were embarked upon, as well as a series of specials exploiting such stars as Nazimova, Viola Dana, May Allison and Bert Lytell.

The company had gained control of many Exchanges, but the problem of the theatres had still to be solved. Rubin and Rowland approached Marcus Loew, then an owner of an important theatre circuit, and Loew, who wanted a steady flow of films for his cinemas, bought out Metro in January 1919. It was none too soon, for Metro was facing disaster. Its weekly receipts had dropped from $108,000 to $6,000, and it was committed to the expensive production of Capellani's *The Red Lantern* with Nazimova.

For his new production company Loew paid over $3 million. His purchases included the new Metro Studio at Cahuenga Boulevard and Romaine Street in

SHORE ACRES, *Metro 1920. Edward Connelly.*

Hollywood. It was here that Ingram was to make some of his most famous films.

The result of the new financial injection was that Loew announced a schedule of films for the coming year, which was to include fifty to seventy-five items to be made at a cost of $20,000 each. These included *The Heart of a Child* with Nazimova, *Alias Jimmy Valentine* with Bert Lytell, *Shore Acres* with Alice Lake and Frank Brownlee, and an unheralded piece called *The Four Horsemen of the Apocalypse*.

As we have seen, *Shore Acres* fell to Ingram and production began — not auspiciously, however. Shooting had gone on for eight days and Ingram refused to pass the scenes as satisfactory. The cameraman was Steve Norton. This could not but make trouble between Ingram and the company. Maxwell Karger already thought that Ingram, though talented, was unmanageable and eccentric and it would have been merely normal to fire him. Karger, however, to his great credit called in John Seitz, a distinguished cameraman, who had begun as a chemist and laboratory man. For some reason Ingram got on well with Seitz and he was to photograph all Ingram's future films with the exception of three. Elmo Lincoln once told Rex that Seitz was too young and inexperienced, but Rex countered this with: 'If he is too young and inexperienced, so am I. I'm not much older than he is.' Phil Rosen who had worked with Ingram as a cameraman tackled Seitz: 'How can you get along with the crazy Irishman. You must be a miracle man.' But there it was. Ingram and Seitz could work hand in glove.

Ingram had seen Seitz's work on *The Westerners*, made previously for Hodkinson, and admired its modelling. Seitz has given a fascinating account of those first days' work with Ingram:

We were to look at part of the eight days' work on the following morning and then resume shooting the picture in the afternoon. We worked about five hours that afternoon and made many set-ups. After we finished, Ingram said he liked the way I worked and the form and modelling he saw in the lighting — as you know he was a sculptor. We had a rush print made, to be seen early in the morning before resuming work on the set. He saw the print before I did, but the effect on the screen he felt was rather harsh and contrasty.

We both went in to see Mr Karger, who suggested we do an exterior sequence on the beach and make a test of an interior scene when we returned to the studio that evening. Before leaving for the location, I asked Mr Ingram if I could look at the still pictures, so we went to his residence and looked at about a hundred still pictures. [Mr Seitz is referring to still pictures from previous pictures Ingram had made.] He did not find a single picture amongst them that he liked, so I felt I was really facing a stone wall but was hopeful that perhaps some light might break through before too long. Fortunately conditions at the ocean were very good, we had excellent surf and clouds and so were able to obtain some very good seascapes. We made the interior test that evening, using substantially the same lighting as the previous day. I developed these myself as I was a former laboratory man, reducing the developing time about twenty per cent from the standard. We did more interiors the following day and then ran the landscapes and test that evening. The exteriors were truly good — even Ingram enthused about them. The interiors were better, but not quite what they could be, in his estimation, so I made another test that evening using the same type of lighting substantially as on the two previous occasions. I also developed these, cutting another twenty per cent off the developing time — making a total of forty per cent — that is from eight minutes to five minutes. On running these the following evening Rex Ingram·said he had for the first time seen an interior scene on the screen which he liked. He asked Mr Karger who was still in the studio, to look at the tests. After Karger saw them he said: 'Now I know what you were after — *light effects*.' Rex replied, 'No, Max, I just wanted some good stuff — and this is it.'

This fascinating insight into Ingram's painstaking method of working reveals the high standards and hard work.

In filming this old stage favourite, Ingram had a subject which appealed to him. He was fond of the sea and liked Laguna Beach because it reminded him of Ireland. He also did some of his shooting for the film at San Pedro. His leading role was played by Alice Lake, a Brooklyn girl who had played in Fatty Arbuckle comedies and had become a Metro star. She later acted with Valentino in *Uncharted Seas*. Edward Connelly, an experienced actor, played the sympathetic brother and was to be a familiar figure in later Ingram films. But most significant of all was the presence of a young girl called Alice Taaffe whom Ingram made a star, fell in love with, and married.

Another important member of the Ingram team was Grant Whytock, a film editor who had worked with von Stroheim on *The Devil's Passkey* and had also cut Rex's *Under Crimson Skies*. Whytock was dissatisfied with the general standards of Universal and when Rex went to Metro he went with him.

Shore Acres told the story of two brothers who tended a lighthouse, of their struggle to retain their piece of land against a grasping speculator and of the love of a young girl for a worthy but penniless suitor. It was released on 28 March 1920 and ran to five reels. A critical success, it was regarded as a very good dramatic film and praised for its fine location work on a rocky coastline, for its realistic interiors and for the best sea storm to date.' The acting received honourable mention. More important for Ingram, Marcus Loew thought very highly of it. Cosmo Hamilton, the British novelist, wrote to *Motion Picture World* as follows: 'I am constrained to send you a few lines to say how deeply impressed and moved I was by Rex Ingram's production of *Shore Acres*: to my mind it is a tender, most masterly and imaginative translation to the screen of that fine old play which has become almost a national institution in the country, and James Herne himself, could he see his characters brought to life as Ingram has revitalised them, would, I am sure, be thrilled as I was. There is great beauty in the picture and all the good emotions. The sea storm makes one hang on to one's chair, and the beautiful symbolism of the lighthouse, so religious in its duty to the men who go down to the sea in ships, is inspiring and noble. Altogether the Metro is to be congratulated on this splendid thing.' Hamilton was to write the story for Rex's second last film *The Three Passions*

HEARTS ARE TRUMPS, *Metro 1920. Alice Terry in her first starring role.*

in 1929.

The next project was the Drury Lane melodrama *Hearts Are Trumps* and here Rex had the scriptwriting services of June Mathis who played an important part in Ingram's career. Alice Terry, the former Alice Taaffe, was promoted to the role of leading lady. Francelia Billington was lured from Universal to play Lady Winifred and other players included Winter Hall, Joseph Kilgour, Frank Brownlee and Edward Connelly. The Seitz-Whytock team worked closely with Ingram.

The story had the usual ingredients of melodrama: long-lost parents, disparate marriages between rich and poor, upheavals of nature. The scenes ranged from England to Switzerland, from stately home to monastery garden. The latter scenes were shot at Capistrano.

When released on 12 September 1920 the film received favourable notices. Its Swiss scenes, its English atmosphere and the setting of the Royal Academy were well done and its lighting and photography were generally on a high level. Alice Terry was much admired; one critic noted that Francelia Billington showed no sign of ageing over a period of twenty years.

With these two films Ingram had pleased the authorities at Metro. *Shore Acres* was the first film of the company to be shown in a large cinema, and *Hearts Are Trumps* reinforced Ingram's reputation. With his next film he was to soar to the top of his profession and become one of the most important directors of his time.

The author of the novel *The Four Horsemen of the Apocalypse* was a Spaniard, Vicente Blasco Ibáñez. A bitter opponent of German war aims, he endeavoured to involve Spain in supporting the Allies. In books like *Mare Nostrum*, he aimed largely at a popular international market. A colourful character, Blasco Ibáñez was born in Valencia on 29 January 1867. Involved in law, journalism and politics, he was also fond of travel, wandering all over Europe, and even founding colonies in Tierra del Fuego and in the tropical forests of Paraguay. His baiting of King Alfonso XIII once led him into trouble. Notorious for his adventures and love affairs he was a man of considerable talent and his early naturalistic novels such as *Flor de Mayo* and *La Barraca* have an honoured place in Spanish literature. By 1920 the *Four Horsemen of the Apocalypse* had become a best-seller in America, and was noticed by the head of Metro's script department, Miss June Mathis.

This remarkable lady was born of theatrical parents in Leadville on 30 June, 1892. Following in her parents profession, she also took up writing, and was attracted to the new medium of the cinema. Edwin Carewe, a Metro director, saw her work and she was engaged to write the scenarios of such currently popular films as *To Hell with the Kaiser, Draft 258* and *The Millionaire's Double* (with Lionel Barrymore). But she wanted to get away from the scenario department and become a producer. She was determined to bring *The Four Horsemen of the Apocalypse* to the screen, and interviewed Blasco Ibáñez while he was on a visit to Chicago.

The whole project of *The Four Horsemen of the Apocalypse* was dramatic. Rowland, President of Metro, was not unaware of the enormous success of the novel. He was in two minds about it. A first attempt to acquire it fell through. Then Jack Meador, a press agent for Metro, raised the matter once more. Blasco

THE FOUR HORSEMEN OF THE APOCALYPSE, *Metro 1921. During shooting. Valentino third from left. Behind wheelchair, June Mathis (left) and Alice Terry. John Seitz beside camera. Ingram in foreground.*

Above: *Ingram instructs Valentino.*
Opposite: *Alice Terry and Valentino rehearse the tango.*

Ibáñez was in Chicago and there was a rumour that the Fox Film Corporation was willing to pay $75,000. Rowland finally got the rights for Metro by paying an advance of $20,000 against ten per cent of the royalties. June Mathis, who had pressed for the film, was asked to write the script and take charge of production. Edwin Carewe had been mentioned as director, but she asked for, and got, Rex Ingram.

June Mathis joined Maxwell Karger in the East after breaking in Bayard Veiller to take her place in Hollywood. But not before it was agreed that the Blasco Ibáñez story should be filmed. After much indecision the project was shelved at one stage only to be resurrected again to meet contract agreements. It was now decided that June Mathis and Ingram were to make the film on the West Coast. Her literary gifts, combination of dramatic experience, and aptitude for pictorial expression suited her vocation in films. She also worked well with Ingram who shared these qualities.

Many players had been considered for the part of Julio, the playboy hero, among them Carlyle Blackwell, Rod la Rocque, Antonio Moreno and Francis MacDonald. June Mathis, with Ingram's support, held out for the young and inexperienced Rudolph Valentino.

This Italian emigré had pursued a career as dancer and screen actor without any marked success. He had appeared in many films in comparatively minor roles, very often as a villain. It is difficult to say exactly who discovered him but it looks as if both Mathis and Ingram can claim the honour. Valentino himself gives the discovery to June Mathis who had seen him in *The Eyes of Youth* with Clara Kimball Young in which he played the heavy. Valentino himself, when he heard the Blasco Ibáñez novel was to be filmed, went to New York to find June Mathis, while she in her turn was looking for him. Eventually he met her in Hollywood and got the part at a contract of $100 a week.

In Samuel Goldwyn's *Behind the Screen* Ingram tells how, when he returned to Hollywood from the Royal Canadian Air Force, he went to a party at a Mr Cole's. Valentino was there with Paul Troubetskoy.

> I was attracted at once by Valentino's face and by his remarkable grace of movement. There's a fellow, I thought, who would be great in pictures, and if I get my job of directing back I'm going to use him . . . No sooner had I started to work than I discovered Valentino on the same lot under Holubar. This second contact with the young foreigner deepened my confidence that he would be a great success on the silver sheet, and when *The Four Horsemen* came along I thought of him immediately. Of course it was obvious that he was the exact type for the young tango-hero of the story. Even after I started with him, though, I had no idea how far he'd go — not at the very first. But, when he came to rehearsing the tango, Rudy did so well that I made up my mind to expand this phase of the story. I did this by means of a sequence in a Universal picture I had made many years ago. The sequence showed an adventurous youth going into a Bowery dive and taking the dancer after he had floored her partner. Bones and marrow I transposed this action to South America — yet only a few of my wise Universal friends recognised it.

The story of *The Four Horsemen* began in the Argentine and told of the return of two branches of a wealthy family to Europe, one to Germany and the other to France. The pleasure-loving central character seduces the wife of one of his father's friends but eventually fights for France when the war comes. His German cousins are fighting on the other side. The erring wife returns to her husband, now blinded in the war. Julio, the hero, is killed. Behind horrors of war and specifically the brutality of the Germans, a mystical theme prevails. The scenes of Parisian life and the depiction of invasion and war made for spectacle and vivid action, and Ingram took full advantage of the variety of plot and character.

Shooting began on 20 July 1920 and lasted six months. Not since Griffith's great epics of *Birth of a Nation* and *Intolerance* had Hollywood seen anything like it.

The casting of the players was of vital importance for this story and much test footage was taken of the various candidates. Ingram had a flair for developing character and, in fact, preferred the human moments of his films to the more spectacular aspects. According to Grant Whytock he used to say about the extras in the crowd scenes 'When can we get rid of them so I can do the personal story?' But in handling crowds few had his equal.

Ingram liked working with people he knew and he used the same players over and over again in his films. He also had a capacity for visualising the character he wished to depict on the screen, and would make a drawing and send his assistants out to find that person. His use of dwarfs and hunchbacks in his films sprang partly from his superstitious belief that they would bring him luck.

The choice of Valentino for the role of the hero, Julio Desnoyers, was more than justified. He was a hard-working conscientious actor. When Ingram first met him he was wearing a moustache. This was soon removed. He was consumed with an ambition to succeed. His earlier experiences in America had been harsh. His particular friend at the time was the actor Norman Kerry. Cosmo Hamilton in his book *Unwritten History* tells of seeing the young Valentino at Leslie Stuart's studio in New York:

> Among these, many of whom had the satisfaction of seeing their names in electric lights, was a quiet fur-coated young man who wanted to sing but had no voice, wanted to act but was without experience, and finally wanted to dance which he did extremely well. Day after day he hung about the Studio, more and more wistful, more and more eager, more and more inarticulate, but never any less glossy of hair or furred of overcoat. What happened to him after realising that a Caruso voice does not come to men by wishing or that an English accent by eating cold roast beef, I haven't the faintest idea. The next time I saw him was when, no longer in a fur-lined overcoat, he played the hero in *The Four Horsemen of the Apocalypse* and made the name of Rudolph Valentino turn the hearts of every woman over twelve and under sixty-five.

Under Ingram's sensitive direction he blossomed into one of the greatest stars of the silent cinema.

Alice Terry was chosen for the role of Marguerite Laurier, a woman torn between love and duty and the ethereal beauty which she irradiates in the film is as striking today as when the film first appeared over fifty years ago. (May Allison had at one stage also been considered for this part.)

John Sainpolis played the injured husband, and the father of Julio was taken by Joseph Swickard, an actor with twenty-five years experience of the stage and ten of films.

Other players included Alan Hale, Nigel de Brulier, Stuart Holmes, Wallace Beery, Jean Hersholt and Edward Connelly. In an extra role was Ramon Samaniegos, an ambitious young Mexican, who apparently attracted no particular notice from Ingram but later stepped into Valentino's shoes under the better-known name of Ramon Novarro.

For Ingram the personal story was the heart of the film and this was shot first, long before the battle scenes. According to Grant Whytock, June Mathis and Ingram did not keep adding to the original script and the personal story was one and a half hours when projected.

The more elaborate scenes were spread over much of Hollywood. The century-old Gilmore Ranch, La Brea, belonging to A. P. Gilmore, an oil magnate, was used for the South American scenes. In the hills behind Griffith Park, today part of Warner Brothers' lot and partly a cemetery, the castle and

THE FOUR HORSEMEN OF THE APOCALYPSE, *Metro 1921. The Centaur rides.*

THE FOUR HORSEMEN OF THE APOCALYPSE, *Metro 1921. The Uhlan cavalry enter the shattered village.*

THE FOUR HORSEMEN OF THE APOCALYPSE, *Metro 1921. Nigel de Brulier as the Mystic with Bowditch Turner and Valentino.*

the village were constructed for $25,000. This alone cost as much as many a previous Metro film. In this setting took place the arrival of the Uhlan cavalry before the French village and the heroic defence by the inhabitants. It is one of the most impressive scenes in the film. Fourteen cameras were used for the scene and many assistant directors took part. One of the most important was Curt Rehfeld, who had served in the German army during the war and who now trained the thousands of extras with Teutonic thoroughness. He was an important member of the Ingram team for many years.

The minimum of battle scenes were filmed, though extensively covered by many cameras. A great deal of this was eliminated in editing.

In shooting the film, Ingram worked very closely with John Seitz. He liked initiative in his collaborators. There was a great deal of mutual respect between these two. As Seitz put it: 'Ingram was a great critic. Intuition told me from the first day that I'd better make the set-up and let him correct it. And so I had the script; I knew the script as well as he did, as I do in all my films. I had to read the script very carefully to get the feeling. This was our relationship. He was shrewd. He wanted the best from me and the best from the art directors and everybody. And he got it. By being an expert critic . . . He knew what he was doing. He wanted the best out of everybody and got it. He was rather unique as far as directors go.'

Whytock says that he never had much difficulty in editing Ingram's films because the coverage was extensive and Ingram understood enough about the requirements of editing. A great deal of footage was discarded and sequences on which the director had worked very hard were often removed to make for a more fluid and perfect story-line. 'Rex's complaint about me was mostly he'd say "Tell me. Give me a warning of what you're going to take out." He said, "I don't like this big surprise." At first I'd say, "Well, let me take it down a little way, and if you don't like it we'll put it back." He'd say, "You'd better warn me a little bit — this is too big a shock." Because we'd take out a whole reel, sometimes a sequence, he'd worked on . . . I guess it would be a great shock to a director to go in suddenly and see a whole piece missing that he had taken a week and a half to direct, or even two weeks. I found him very easy to understand.'

Sometimes, if a shot was not satisfactory from the editing point of view, Ingram would have no hesitation about re-shooting it. He was a perfectionist in all things and checked every detail of set and camera set-up. Whytock recalls seeing him repaint a set if he didn't like it, move pictures about on walls and re-arrange everything on the set. 'Everything had to make composition to him.'

A *Moving Picture World* correspondent describes the making of the battle scenes: 'I went out to the hills beyond Griffith Park over a switchback automobile road to where Rex Ingram is making the battle stuff for Metro's *Four Horsemen*. This is one of the most elaborate things of its kind I have ever seen. There was a French village built up on a slope of a hill and across the canyon, a castle with walls over 200 ft high. The scene represented a part of the battle of the Marne. The German army was approaching and throwing shells into the town.

'The village was made on the breakaway system. A telephone switchboard, with lines running to more than a hundred points of the village was used to direct the demolition of the buildings. The firing of a battery some way back somewhere in the hill would start, Ingram would phone "Breakaway No. 25" and a roof would cave in with a burst of flame.

'Another minute and part of the steeple of the church would come down with a mighty crash. Next the front of a shop would come tumbling into the street. Then the big siren that was used for signalling the battery would screech its 'stop firing' signal and things would be quiet until the smoke cleared away . . .'

The official statistics of the production show that it cost $1 million and took six months to make. Twelve thousand people were engaged. There were fourteen cameramen, twelve assistant directors, five million feet of raw film were exposed, 125 tons of steel, timber, masonry, shrubbery and furniture were used.

A particular problem arose with the effect of the symbolic horsemen who

Overleaf: THE FOUR HORSEMEN OF THE APOCALYPSE, *Metro 1921*.
Valentino the Latin lover.

represent Conquest, War, Famine and Death. This visionary scene is one of the most effective in the film and was worked out by Ingram in close co-operation with his art directors and cameramen. The scene was shot on Pico Boulevard and positive film was used for high contrast. A hole 3 feet deep was dug in the road for a low-angle shot.

On 8 January 1921 the *Moving Picture World* reported that the last editing had been completed. Towards the end of February a private showing was given to the cinema and literary notables at the Ritz Carlton Hotel New York. At the same hour a private showing was arranged for Vicente Blasco Ibáñez at Nice. The showings indicated a film of considerable stature and everyone conceded the mastery of its presentation. But the question still remained — how would it fare at the box-office? It was a war film and people were tired of war. Marcus Loew was none too sure. He found the film too long and involved.

THE FOUR HORSEMEN OF THE APOCALYPSE, *Metro 1921. The shadow of war threatens the lovers. Valentino and Alice Terry.*

But there was no need to worry. The film opened at the Lyric Theatre, New York, on 6 March 1921, where it was presented by Dr Hugo Riesenfeld with full orchestral and sound effects. It was an immediate success. Valentino took the American public by storm. Alice Terry, looking beautiful and gracious, had an almost equal triumph while Ingram leaped straightaway into the Griffith-de Mille class as a director. Marcus Loew had backed a winner, which won for him more than the total purchase price of the Metro studios. It put the company back on the map as a going concern.

It was now clear that a major picture was born and Richard Rowland who was in Europe seeking rights in the new Jacques Feyder sensation *L'Atlantide* took it upon himself to call on Blasco Ibáñez in Menton, where the writer was living in exile at the Villa Rosa. He offered to buy back Ibáñez's rights for $170,000, an offer which was accepted. On his return to the States Rowland found that according to the original agreement Metro would have had to pay the

THE FOUR HORSEMEN OF THE APOCALYPSE, *Metro 1921. Alice Terry and Valentino.*

author $210,000. The film was cleaning up at the box-office and its gross earnings up to the end of 1925 were about $4 million. It is somewhat ironic that Rowland never bothered to read the novel.

The film was a world sensation and long before it travelled abroad it was written about, talked about and eagerly awaited. In April it transferred to the Astor Theatre in New York. A private viewing was arranged for President Harding in May. In September, official Washington saw a special showing.

Its presentation was on a lavish scale wherever it went. Lee Lawrie, Ingram's old sculpture teacher at Yale, designed special large cut-outs for the cinemas showing the film, and he also executed a sculptural group of the Four Horsemen.

In spite of the clamouring demand for the film in Europe some considerable time elapsed before it crossed the Atlantic. It opened at the Palace Theatre, London, as late as 14 August 1922. It reached Ingram's native Dublin in January of 1923 where a savage attack by a narrow-minded sectarian press did not lessen its popularity.

The impact was immediate. First of all the scope of the production was impressive. Equally effective were the performances of the players. The rich subtle photography by John Seitz brought a quality to the film which equalled that of the German productions which were then being heard of in America. Ingram's direction, in spite of the biassed caricaturing of the Germans, had a sophisticated quality which was far from the naive canvasses of Griffith. The research and care brought to the film are best seen in the sense of location and period. The streets of Paris, the war hysteria, the terrors of invasion, the horrors of the battlefield, the faithful depiction of social milieus and the mystical tension binding the story together made for a film of overwhelming excitement. The scenes at Lourdes, the visions of the mystic Tchernoff, when he sees the apocalyptic vision, and the impressive final scene in the war cemetery with its rows of white crosses against the horizon as Tchernoff says 'I knew them all' and vanishes from the scene, drew audiences seeking comfort from the horrors through which they had passed. Above all the poignancy of the love scenes between Valentino and Alice Terry displayed a sensitivity rare to screen acting of that time.

Ingram who specialised in depicting exotic locations in his earlier films here created a Europe in the throes of war — an achievement all the more remarkable in that he had lived all his life in Ireland and America. His sense of scholarship and research and his fidelity to detail are stamped all over the picture.

The film moved into the category of a great classic of the screen and wherever repertories of film history are screened it is always included. If it is the name of Valentino which draws the audiences it is the achievement of Ingram which finally remains in the mind. It is today preserved in film archives as far flung as Moscow and Buenos Aires.

In spite of slight departures from the novel, particularly in the discovery of the wife's infidelity, the author gave it his blessing: 'It is such a masterful realisation of my novel that I feel I owed a grand debt of gratitude to Mr Ingram for the artistry of his direction. If it were to have been done at all it had to be done on a monumental scale. The acting, too, is of superlative quality. I am particularly indebted to Alice Terry and to Rudolph Valentino for their realisation of my characters of Marguerite and Julie.' This first association of Ingram with Blasco Ibáñez was to lead to a lifelong friendship and a further collaboration between the two men.

Critical opinion was almost universally favourable and any reservations did not diminish the glory of the achievement. The *Moving Picture World* review by Edward Weitzel said: ' . . . it marks the advent of a master craftsman. Rex Ingram, the director of *The Four Horsemen of the Apocalypse*, has by it won a position amongst the leaders of his profession.

'The casting of the characters, the correctness of the locations, the minute perfection of settings and costumes, the sure guess of light effects, the perfect moulding of the human countenance by the proper use of light and shadow, the composition of the individual scenes and the splendid command of form and tempo cannot escape without recognition. The cutting of the picture is practically flawless. By the time it reaches the general public it will have the symmetry of a tone poem. Nothing is more remarkable about this screen epic than its subjection of every element to the laws of true drama, to the elimination of every foot that interferes with the progress of the story.'

Robert Emmett Sherwood, the dramatist, writing in *Life* of 24 March 1921, said: 'The great strength and vigorous appeal with which *The Four Horsemen of the Apocalypse* has been endowed is largely due to the superb direction of Rex Ingram, who produced it. His was a truly Herculean task, and he has done it so well that his name must now be placed at the top of his profession . . .

'The pictures themselves are at all times striking, and occasionally beautiful — for Ingram has evidently studied closely the art of composition, and almost any scene taken at random from the nine reels would be worthy of praise for its pictorial qualities alone . . .

'Comparisons are necessarily odious, but we cannot help looking back over the brief history of the Cinema and find something that can be compared with *The Four Horsemen of the Apocalypse*. The films which first come to mind are *The Birth of a Nation, Intolerance, Hearts of the World* and *Joan the Woman*; but the grandiose posturings of D. W. Griffith and Cecil B. de Mille appear pale and artificial in the light of this new production, made by a company which has never been rated very high. Nor does the legitimate stage come out entirely unscathed in the test of comparison, for this mere movie easily surpasses the noisy claptrap which passes off as art in the box-office of the Belasco Theatre . . .

'*The Four Horsemen of the Apocalypse* is a living breathing answer to those who still refuse to take motion pictures seriously. Its production lifts the silent drama to an artistic plane that it has never touched before.' These two reviews are typical of the appreciation and praise that the film earned from the critics.

There are some items of interest in connection with the production that deserve mention. Rex displayed the persistence of von Stroheim in his handling of the military scenes, where every costume had to be authenticated, and his adviser on military matters was his brother Colonel F. C. Hitchcock. Furthermore his assistant Curt Rehfeld drilled the make-believe German armies for hours each day until they were experts in the goose-step. The designers were Amos Myers and Joseph Calder, the former being an old school friend from

THE FOUR HORSEMEN OF THE APOCALYPSE, *Metro 1921. The war cemetery.*

Yale. Ramon Novarro appeared in the scene where the French officers gather around the spirit of France. In that same scene, Ingram used colour effects for the flag and in another scene where Marguerite holds a rose it appears in natural colours.

In those days dupe negs were of poor quality and, as scenes were shot from several cameras, Grant Whytock prepared three negatives from which prints were taken. One of the prints is two reels shorter than the others due to the lack of material for that particular negative.

Valentino's salary had grown to $350 a week during the production. He worked hard and took an interest in everything that went on, even going out to Griffith Park to watch the big scenes, in which he did not appear, being shot. He took direction well and Ingram brought out all his Latin charm and sophistication. He loved every moment of his publicity. There is an amusing story that Ingram found him one day at the back of the set arranging to pose on a horse for some news cameraman. Ingram noticed that he had put the horse's saddle on back to front and saw to it that he didn't pose for unauthorised photos again.

Rex himself was not averse to publicity. He was credited as the film's producer and had precedence in the billings. He was jealous of his rights in this matter and had photographers take pictures in cinema lobbies to indicate whether his name was properly billed.

While *The Four Horsemen* was having its successful première in New York, affairs in Ireland were going from bad to worse, and the dreadful civil war which was to affect his father in no small degree, was brewing. In New York, Sir Philip Gibbs was lecturing at the Casino Theatre on 'The Irish Situation' and again at Carnegie Hall, where the chairman was his half-brother, Cosmo Hamilton, Ingram's friend. Hamilton records that the large audience of Irish present were 'in a state of hysterical rage' and one Father Duffy had to appeal for calm so that the speaker could be heard.

When the shooting of *The Four Horsemen* concluded in December, Valentino went off to Catalina to play in Wesley Ruggles' production of *Uncharted Seas* with Alice Lake, the heroine of Ingram's *Shore Acres.* Sol Polito, who was proposed as an alternative to Seitz for *Shore Acres,* was the cameraman on the new Valentino film, but was replaced by Seitz, whom Ingram loaned while he was preparing his next film, an updated version of Balzac's *Eugénie Grandet.*

Curiously *The Four Horsemen* was not Ingram's favourite film, though his editor thought it his best. Seitz was particularly proud of his own work on it.

A drawing by Ingram for THE FOUR HORSEMEN OF THE APOCALYPSE.

The Irish Civil War as Ingram saw it.

6 Combined Operations

The enormous success of *The Four Horsemen of the Apocalypse* had so raised the status of Ingram at the Metro Studios that he virtually had *carte blanche* in his future operations. *The Conquering Power,* based on Balzac's *Eugénie Grandet* was a small-scale story of intimate passions far removed from the spectacular range of his previous film.

Valentino and Alice Terry had more than justified his belief in them, and they were once more given the leads. Ingram now had a well-established team of collaborators. His cameraman John Seitz, and his editor Grant Whytock worked well with him, and he with them. The cameraman is the eye of the director, and the director-camera teams have been a characteristic in the history of the cinema — Griffith and Billy Bitzer, James Cruze and Karl Brown, Eisenstein and Tisse.

Ingram planned the sets of the new film with his former fellow-student from Yale, Ralph Barton, a poster artist. In directing this picture Ingram insisted on his players speaking French to help them get the feel of their environment. Ralph Lewis, a very fine character actor, played the role of the miser Grandet and Edward Connelly was the notary Cruchet.

It was a very free adaptation of the Balzac story with considerable modernisation and re-shuffling of character and incident. In this tale of a miser who would destroy his daughter's happiness and separate her from her lover, Ingram was working within an enclosed area of human activity. He peopled his tiny canvas with characters exhibiting eccentricities of behaviour which interested him particularly, and time and time again the camera of John Seitz caught nuances of life through narrow doorways or corridors, in gloomy rooms, attics and cellars. The film is full of mood and atmosphere, soul-destroying and claustrophobic, stark and grotesque.

Above all it rendered homage to Ingram's great idol, D. W. Griffith, whom he regarded as his master, as did so many other intelligent and devoted directors. In this film the patient and long-suffering Alice Terry is very much a Lillian Gish heroine. Even her hands express their tormented feelings in close-up. Above the symbolic rocking cradle a tall narrow window sends down its shaft of light bringing us back to that key-shot from Griffith's *Intolerance*.

But the most interesting comparison is with von Stroheim, who, we remember, was a friend of Ingram, the one person in Hollywood he admired and trusted. Von Stroheim thought highly of Ingram's work and two years later he elaborated the same theme in the masterpiece, *Greed*. In both films gold is a corroding and destroying influence. In the original version of *Greed*, which was forty reels long, hallucination plays a large part and in the symbolic

THE CONQUERING POWER, *Metro 1921. Ralph Lewis as Père Grandet.*

THE CONQUERING POWER, *Metro 1921. The village. John George wheeling the barrow.*

THE CONQUERING POWER, *Metro 1921. Ralph Lewis, Edward Connelly and Alice Terry.*

sequences of the film gold is shown as a living evil presence. In the very powerful scene where Grandet is trapped in his locked strong-room and feels it closing in to destroy him, the cradle of gold comes alive, breathing and sending up gaunt grasping hands to draw the miser into it. Later in *Greed*, von Stroheim was to use such scenes. There is, too, a suggestion of perverse eroticism in *The Conquering Power* just as in the scene in *Greed* where Trina pours the gold coins over her naked body.

There are many points of interest in the Ingram film — for instance the introduction of an Arab motif in the scene where young Grandet is enjoying the pleasures of Paris high life. An elaborate tent is incorporated in the design of the great hall where this scene occurs. Ingram's future concern with the life of North Africa may be foreshadowed here. The feeling of decay in Grandet's old house is particularly skilfully depicted. Details, such as the spider walking over the dusty stolen letters of Eugénie, reinforce the mood of the film. Valentino, in a less dominant role than Julio, shows an improvement in his

THE CONQUERING POWER, *Metro 1921. Valentino and Alice Terry.*

THE CONQUERING POWER, *Metro 1921. Paris High Life.*

acting while the well-known charm is never far absent. He is also superbly photographed, but it is very much Alice Terry's picture.

The film opened in New York at the Tivoli Theatre on 3 July 1921 to a paean of praise from the critics. The *New York Times* regarded it as one of the best films ever to reach Broadway. It praised Ingram's direction, but suggested that he should look for material outside literary sources and find someone who could write directly for the film. This of course puts its finger on a perennial problem of the cinema, and on a particular weakness of Ingram's. Original scriptwriters who are not mere adaptors, and who could compose solely in terms of film images, have always been rare. The German, Carl Mayer, for example, has had few rivals in the history of the cinema, and the number of directors who provided their own material can be numbered on one hand.

But generally the critics admired the new film which reminded them of the German films becoming familiar at the time. P. F. Renier in the *New York*

Ingram at Yale for conferring of honorary degree.

Evening Post comments: 'It has an ease of continuity that is soothing in effect; the tone shadings of its photography seem equivalent to the elusive quality of sensuous music; and Mr Ingram's groups fall, dissolve and fall again into pictures so well composed that one regrets the necessity for continuous movement. These qualities make *The Conquering Power* a film that will bear seeing not only once but several times, and we make bold to recommend it to those, if any, who are still sceptical of the screen as an instrument of beauty.' Harriet Underhill of the *New York Tribune* referred to: 'the splendid direction of this man Ingram . . . particularly now, when so much is being felt about the German films, is such a picture welcome. Germany has turned out nothing finer.' New York's *Evening Mail* regarded it as 'a distinct contribution to the evolution of motion picture production'.

From about the time of the famous *Cabinet of Dr Caligari* of 1919, the artistic development of the German cinema had been remarkable. The brilliant camerawork and design, the emergence of great players like Jannings, Werner Krauss, Conrad Veidt, Paul Wegener, Pola Negri, Henny Porten and others were causing a stir in artistic circles. Despite the recent war German films were beginning to conquer the prejudices of America. That Ingram's films were being judged by the same high standards and comparing favourably indicates his position in the film industry.

Unlike his previous production, however, all did not run smoothly. There were various causes of discontent. Valentino has received no financial increase in salary since *The Four Horsemen.* He was no longer just another actor, but a nation's ideal. He had formed an attachment for the designer Natacha Rambova, a young woman of independent means, who decided she was going to run the young man's life and his affairs. Under her influence he became less amenable to direction and produced ideas of his own, particularly in relation to his dress. There were tearful scenes and mighty rows as Ingram was not the man to be crossed. June Mathis, undoubtedly in love with Valentino, resented Ingram's script changes which did not favour her idol. It is not at all impossible that she was also in love with Ingram himself, but received small encouragement from that direction. At one stage Valentino walked out of the film, but was persuaded to come back.

Valentino presented Maxwell Karger with a demand for $450 a week, representing an increase of $100. Karger merely offered him an increase of $50. Indignant at this treament, Valentino approached Jesse Lasky of Paramount and told him of his dissatisfaction with Metro. Lasky realising the potentialities and vitality of Valentino put him straightaway on a five-year contract of $500 a week. Although they didn't get on there was a little real hard feeling between Valentino and Ingram. When Valentino visited Europe some years later, Ingram who was then in Nice welcomed his old star, although with some reservations.

When Valentino left Metro for Paramount, June Mathis went with him — a double loss. But Metro still regarded Ingram as their major asset.

At the end of the shooting of *The Conquering Power,* Yale University conferred an honorary degree of Bachelor of Arts on Ingram in appreciation of his creative work. To enable him to get to Yale in time for the conferring of the degree, *The Conquering Power* was shot, with everyone's co-operation, in five weeks. It was the first of many honours he was to receive. I think he always coveted academic distinctions and must have regretted that he could not continue his early Yale studies. The consistent spread of the rumour that he was educated in Trinity College cannot have been entirely without his connivance.

While *The Conquering Power* was a *succes d'estime* it was not a great box-office triumph. It was re-released, however, on 25 September 1926, a few weeks after Valentino's death.

The next film Ingram was to direct owed much to Marcus Loew than to its maker. Loew liked *Turn to the Right* a play by Winchell Smith which had a huge Broadway success. With John Golden, he paid $250,000 for a half-share of the rights. Ingram wasn't keen on the story, but tackled it when asked to direct. The author wished the filming to be done on his estate in Connecticut, but it was finally shot entirely on the West Coast. Ingram wanted Cullen Landis for the lead; Raymond Hatton was also under consideration. Eventually,

TURN TO THE RIGHT, *Metro 1921. Alice Terry and Jack Mulhall.*

however, his old acquaintance from Edison days, Jack Mulhall, played the hero with Alice Terry, Edward Connelly, Harry Myers, George Cooper and Lydia Knott in the other roles.

The story tells of one Joe Bascom, in love with Elsie, daughter of Dean Tillinger. He leaves his native village to make his fortune. He becomes a groom at a racing stable, but is then imprisoned on a charge put up by his employer's son. Meanwhile Tillinger is trying to get hold of Mrs Bascom's farm. Joe returns with two fellow prisoners, who manage to steal money from Tillinger to pay off loans for Joe's mother. The man who framed Joe is unmasked and his employer gives him back with interest the money he was supposed to have stolen. With this Joe turns his mother's farm into a prosperous jam-making enterprise and marries Elsie. His two friends are provided with wives from the village.

This melodramatic story gave Ingram little to go on. It relied a great deal on crude humour and humour was not one of Ingram's assets. Its highlights were a horse race, underworld scenes, and the exploitation of a peach orchard. The script was taken over from June Mathis by Mary O'Hara, but the film was a disappointment to Ingram enthusiasts and it was being whispered that the real artist behind the Valentino films was Mathis and not Ingram. While he was working on this minor film in October 1921, over one hundred road companies were distributing *The Four Horsemen* and Richard Rowland was in Paris negotiating its French release.

In spite of gossip, Ingram was to have great success with his last film of the year. This was Sir Anthony Hope's popular *The Prisoner of Zenda* which had been filmed in America and Britain in 1913 and 1915 respectively. The new version was based on the novel and partly on Edward Rose's play which began its career at the St James Theatre, London, in 1896. It was an expensive production. The uniforms alone cost $160,000. The reproduction of the Cellini dragon for the helmets was entrusted to a craftsman named Finn Frolich. The sets called for a cathedral, a castle, a hunting-lodge, and the streets of a state capital.

The cast included, of course, Alice Terry as Flavia, Lewis Stone in the dual role of the king and Rasendyll, Stuart Holmes as Black Michael, Robert Edeson as Colonel Sapt, Lois Lee as Countess Helga and Malcolm McGregor as Fritz von Tarlenheim. Last, but by no means least, one Ramon Samaniegos played Rupert of Hentzau.

On the departure of Valentino, Ingram was determined to find a new actor whom he could build up to the heights of stardom. A young dancer and actor named Ramon Samaniegos had appeared in several films including *Omar Khayyam,* a not very successful life of the Persian poet by Ferdinand Pinney Earle. Margaret Loomis, who played in *Turn to the Right* drew Ingram's attention to Samaniegos, then appearing in *The Royal Fandango* in a little theatre in Hollywood. Ingram was impressed with the boy and felt that here was the substitute for Valentino. There were the good looks, grace of movement, the Latin temperament, all allied to real acting ability. Samaniegos was taken under Ingram's wing for grooming as a star and was cast as the dashing villain. He made a hit in the role and became the famous Ramon Novarro of subsequent Ingram films, reaching the peak of his career in the title role of

THE PRISONER OF ZENDA, *Metro 1922. Lewis Stone and Alice Terry.*

Above: THE PRISONER OF ZENDA, *Metro 1922. Ingram directs Novarro and Barbara La Marr.*
Opposite: *Ingram with cast and crew of* THE PRISONER OF ZENDA.

Metro-Goldwyn's *Ben Hur.* Curiously he had failed to arouse any notice as an extra in *The Four Horsemen of the Apocalypse.* He was one of the young officers in the scene where the woman sings the Marseillaise draped in the French tricolour.

The Prisoner of Zenda, the perfect romantic costume drama, is set in an imaginary European kingdom. It has pageantry, swashbuckling action, idealistic self-sacrifice, intrigue and impersonation. It was elaborately mounted by Ingram and the characterisation of the players was good. Yet today its appeal has faded. The script lacks cinematic flow and does not show real grip on the action. There was some trouble too with the editing. Grant Whytock says he stayed up all night working on the sequence where John George climbs up the wall of the castle to get into a room where he plans to strangle Lewis Stone. It does not stand up to the later sound, and probably definitive, version by John Cromwell which had Ronald Colman, Madeleine Carroll and Douglas Fairbanks Junior. (Perhaps it is unfair to compare the silent with the sound version as they are effectively different media.)

Ingram's film was, however, very successful both with the critics and at the box-office. It received extravagant praise which a viewing today tends to discredit. Robert Garland in the *Baltimore American* again makes the comparison with German films: 'It has discernment, humanity and an ever-present sense of

beauty . . . Nowadays when so much is being written and said about the excellence of the German-made film it is heartening to see such a fine American photoplay as this.'

The *New York Times* took a more critical view and found it uneven, lacking in style, marred by crude humour and without the dash such a romantic yarn should have. But it still conceded that it was above average for its day. The film opened in New York at the Astor Theatre on Monday 31 July 1922.

The three films of Ingram we have just mentioned had one thing in common. Alice Terry was the leading lady. In July 1921 Ingram announced his engagement to Miss Terry and on 5 November, during the making of *The Prisoner of Zenda*, they were married in Pasadena. This was a more romantic story than any Ingram directed and deserves a chapter to itself.

Below: *The Metro Studio*
Previous page: THE PRISONER OF ZENDA, *Metro 1922. The coronation scene.*

7 Alice

Alice Frances Taaffe was born in Vincennes, Indiana, on 24 July 1900. She was the daughter of Martin Taaffe and his wife, Ella Thorn. Her father, a farmer, came from County Kildare, Ireland. Her mother had French blood. Alice, a bright child with auburn hair and blue eyes, was the youngest of three children. The others were Edna, who was to be a close companion to her in later years, and a brother.

In 1904 the family moved to Los Angeles, where Martin Taaffe was tragically killed in a street accident. The others returned to Indiana shortly afterwards, and Alice began school. A year later, however, they arrived back in Los Angeles and Alice enrolled at Grand Avenue School. Her constant companion at the time was a little black girl who lived nearby. Eventually the Taaffes moved to Venice,. California. There life was difficult for them. Sister Edna got a job in a candy store while Alice went to Santa Monica High School. Naturally intense, Alice was nevertheless always full of fun. Enid Markey, the well-established movie actress, who lived in the same building, coaxed Alice to try her luck at Inceville, then a ramshackle community near a stinking fishing village where films were made the hard way. She earned $12 a week and Thomas Ince liked her. Charlotte Arthur, a fellow extra, recalled some years later 'Alice Terry, with whom we at once made friends, whose name was Taaffe in those days and whom everyone called Taffy. She was very poor and very Irish and very simple and nice – and very plump – and nobody thought she had a chance. She couldn't act. Well . . . Rex Ingram taught her to do that.'

She was a gentle, sensitive girl, not pushing enough for the rough and tumble of films. She tried several studios for jobs, but had no great confidence in herself. She started a picture *Free and Equal* about a black man and a white girl with Reginald Barker and Roy Neill, but they didn't like her and gave the role to Gloria Hope. When Ince was there she regained her confidence, but found it difficult to act for others. However she had some success in *Not My Sister* (1916) with Bessie Barriscale and William Desmond. In Ince's spectacular *Civilisation* (1916) although only fifteen she played everything from a peasant to a German soldier.

Along with Valentino, she was an extra for the Universal Company. Later, they acted together in *Alimony* (1918), directed by Emmett Flynn for the Metro Company. So, as leads in *The Four Horsemen* some years later they were not strangers.

Alice decided to give up acting and got a job in the cutting room at Lasky's, but had to give this up because of the bad effect on her health of the fumes of the film cement used in splicing film.

Her meeting with Ingram was the turning point of her life: 'I first met Rex in 1917 — he was making a picture with Henry B. Walthall at the John Brunton Studio. I played an extra for two or three days and then he left for the Royal Flying Corps.' This was at a time when Ingram was very unhappy. His marriage was breaking up and he sorely needed friendship. She goes on: 'I didn't hear from him again until the end of the war. He called one day and said he wanted me to pose for a head he was sculpting. He was very sick at the time and I only posed two or three times. Then I didn't see him for some months and one day I had a call to do extra work as a model in a picture called *The Day She Paid* and Rex was directing. He spoke very harshly to me and I started to cry and I walked off the set and refused to go back. The next morning Rex called for me himself and apologised and said to come back and that soon he was going to change studios and he would have a part for me. I said I would consider a job as a script girl but I was through with acting.'

It was clear that Rex was deeply attracted by Alice at this stage. She remembered what her mother had said about receiving attentions from handsome men, especially film directors. Her attitude was one of cautious interest. She talks humorously about it today. She recalls when on location she and Rex shared adjoining rooms for the night. The door between them could be opened from his side, but not from hers. She sat up all night only to find the next morning that Rex had had a sound night's sleep.

She remembers that in her day the Prince of Wales was supposed to be *the* thing, but that she thought Rex looked much better than he did. When she met him after the war at the junction of Hollywood Boulevard and Highland he was wearing a little cap and a trench-coat which he wore for so long that, later on, Marcus Loew offered him $10,000 to get rid of it.

When Rex went to Metro she had a small part in *Shore Acres* and he was considering her for the *ingenue* in *Hearts are Trumps*. 'I was putting on some make-up one day and there was a blonde wig and I put it on and it looked so silly. Just then Rex came in and said, "Leave that on," and I thought, "Oh no, I can't do that part," but I kept it on. And it felt so silly. We didn't see the rushes for about three days as we were on location. We went into the projection room and I had a terrible headache and I had been taken out of pictures before so I wasn't too confident about myself. When I appeared on the screen I looked so different and from that time on I never got rid of the wig. I was stuck with it. I didn't feel like myself and my freckles didn't seem to show. My skin looked whiter and there was a different person there. If I ever had to rehearse I always put the wig on or I couldn't do it.'

For *Hearts are Trumps*, Alice went on location to Capistrano where scenes were taken in the famous Spanish mission there. Rex was rather possessive about Alice who was fond of playing the ukelele and he resented his assistant director, Walter Mayo, being entertained by her in her room. When filming *The Four Horsemen* originally Alice used to get a streetcar to work which only took her part of the way, after which she had a considerable walk to the studio. A kindly taxi-man who passed her each morning offered to take her direct to the studio for free. One day when Rex heard the taxi-man say, 'Goodbye Alice. I'll see you in the morning.' he said, 'He shouldn't call you Alice, you're going to be a star.' She replied, 'Look, he can call me Alice if he picks me up. I'm

Opposite: *Alice Terry and Rex Ingram at the time of their marriage.*

not going to work on that streetcar and walk six blocks to the studio.' After that Rex saw that she was provided with studio transport.

Looking back, Alice recalls the famous opening night of *The Four Horsemen*: 'I had been working around in films so long from Inceville and I knew everyone in pictures that used to say "Alice, I don't know why you don't get ahead", but nobody put me in anything, you know. So the first night we went to *The Four Horsemen* my mother got me ready and everyone in the house was getting me ready because it was a big to-do down on — I forget the name of the theatre — the Mission Theatre, I think, where it opened in Los Angeles. I'd heard from Rex that it was a big success. He called up and said it was a big success in New York and I went down there and there was complete silence and nobody even looked at me. Some people said "Hello Alice", and I thought, "Well they've heard something that I haven't heard and I'm no good in it", and then at the intermission these people I began to know began to recognise me, but they didn't know I had changed my name and that I had changed so much and that I was blonde and all this, and then it was very exciting. And I still didn't believe it because I thought, "This'll be the end. I've had it. Now it's over but it was good while it lasted".'

To the question 'Were you aware that you had made a success?' she replied, 'No, I was only glad that everybody recognised me. I was only glad because of all these people who had been saying to me "You never do anything". Finally I thought, "Well now they can see", but it never occurred to me that I would ever do anything more.'

Rex had done a very thorough job with his protégé. 'I didn't believe any of it. I was too fat, my hair didn't work, I had to go and have my teeth fixed, I had to wear high-heeled shoes for my ankles, do this, do that, I had to change my name and I finally asked Rex whatever gave him the idea in the first place. I also had to attend a place where I got thin.'

Alice disclaims that she was in love with Rex at this time. A charming friendship existed between the two. They would meet at a Pasadena tearoom (the wild life of Hollywood!) and tell each other of their activites and ambitions. 'Then he would take me home and later everyone on the set would tell me where he had been the night before — all the other girls, you know — and I thought, "Well, good for him". And I kind of liked him but I thought "That's not for me".'

But one evening Rex, Alice and Ralph Barton were walking along the street and Rex asked Alice if she thought they had enough in common to get along. 'And I said, "I think we get along pretty well," and he said "Well, I mean to get married," and he had always told me all this time that he was going to wait till he had so much money before he got married and I knew he didn't have that much. And I thought, "I don't think he wants to marry me, really, and I don't know whether I want to marry him". Then afterwards I thought, "Well, if it doesn't work we could always get a divorce." I really thought that. He said "You won't have to work when we are married", which pleased me.'

One night, shortly after, Alice decided she would cook a meal and she telephoned her mother, her sister and everyone in town to find out how to do it. 'I think I had enough food for forty people. In case one burned I'd have the other and I was all day doing it and Rex came in and ate and said, "This is just marvellous. Why don't we do this every day?" and that was the end of my cooking. Never again!' Perhaps she did not prepare food on so lavish a scale again but she certainly underestimates her capacities as a cook. I can personally vouch for them.

While Alice may have been dependent on Rex, she nevertheless had very definite ideas of her own. She did not really like the *ingenue* roles she played nor did she have a high opinion of the mental ability of the heroines she so beautifully brought to life. When Valentino was cast in the lead role in *The Sheik* at Paramount, Jesse Lasky and George Melford, the director, wanted Alice to play opposite him, but Rex was already planning to cast her in *Turn to the Right*. She does not regret missing this experience.

To return to *The Four Horsemen*. The responsibility of the role of Marguerite was an ordeal for the young actress who was only twenty at the time. 'When I read the book I was terribly frightened and I used to look at those big sets and wish I could run away; but once we started on the work I forgot to be afraid — I was fascinated. We had a wonderful time making that picture. A spirit of cameraderie enveloped the whole company and I'll never forget how good they were, each trying to help me. Mr Ingram took infinite pains to explain what he wanted brought out; Miss Mathis sat on the set and told me the thousand and one things a woman sees in a role such as mine; while Rudie encouraged me every minute. The night of the preview, I was as nervous as if I were making a first· stage appearance and I had enough thrills to last for years to come. As I sat watching the picture, I couldn't believe it was really me there on the screen. Everytime I passed out of a scene I would sink back in my seat and relax, for I was working harder that night than I ever did before the camera. Why, I even cried every time I cried on the screen. I was so ashamed.'

Work was hard on this film. Alice left the house at 5 am. She studied French on the way because as Rex had her learn the spoken dialogue titles of the film in French as he was taking no chances with lip-readers. It was, remember, a silent film. 'And then we'd get on the set and nobody else spoke French except Valentino. And I finally got down to where nobody paid much attention to me — I'd speak a French title, and I learned one very well, and I'd keep speaking the same title. Nobody could tell the difference. But Valentino finally said, "If you say that one more time I'm going to . . ." So then Rex got on to it, and I had to learn the rest.'

Out of it all came that beautiful and moving portrayal of Marguerite Laurier which today has lost none of its power or feeling. Alice's physical beauty and dignity has withstood the ravages of time, an impression reinforced by her portrayals of Eugénie Grandet, Princess Flavia, Aline Kercadiou and Domini Enfilden, but above all by her favourite role of Freya Talberg in *Mare Nostrum*.

Rex was very impressed with her cinematic capabilities. He felt that perhaps people thought he had given her an unfair advantage. He was also appreciative of her other more human qualities. She had a knack of making discreet suggestions not overtly presented by her. Rex's respect for her judgement saved his strong-willed and impetuous personality from making more blunders than he did. 'In my view,' Ingram said, 'she is one of the most versatile women on the screen. Miss Terry's nicely balanced judgement at all times makes her advice to me invaluable not only in the work of directing but also in business . . . If

Alice had been married to someone else when I met her, I think I would promptly have engaged her as my business manager.'

Cleo Madison was an actress whom Ingram admired very much when he directed her films in 1916 — *Black Orchids* and *Chalice of Sorrow*. He found that Alice possessed some of the same qualities. 'I have always directed them both in the same way, that is, by suggesting to them rather than by directing them. Each expresses her emotion with a minimum of effort. Each thinks her role rather than acts it and each has a depth of feeling and a highly sympathetic understanding of the part she plays.'

Willis Goldbeck, later to become one of the most distinguished script writers for Ingram and other directors, has given a pen-picture of Alice: 'Her supreme asset is her complete passivity. She is, before the camera, in absolute subjection to his will. But I think the secret of her lies not in the slim reed of gold beauty she presents to us, so much as in her utter indifference. Off the screen it garbs her completely. It is fascinating as all consistent indifference is fascinating. It seems cold, quite bored. Upon the screen its metamorphosis is remarkable. It becomes that extraordinary poise, wherein there appears to be depth, repose, infinite sympathy.''

Rex's professional interest in Alice did not, as we know, exclude deeper feelings. 'When I came back ill (from the war) and couldn't get a job, Alice used to come to the studio I shared with another amateur sculptor (Elizabeth Waggoner) and talk to me and pose for me. I did two heads of her. Alice asked to hold the script for *Hearts are Trumps*. I wanted her to play the lead. "No, Mr Ingram, I can't. I haven't had enough experience in playing important roles like that." She finally consented. We became quite inseparable pals after that. I always found her wonderful to direct too. I really don't know when we fell in love. "I've always had a crush on you", she said the other day, adding, though with her whimsical little smile, "but then you know I'm a little nutty anyway." She's usually a very dignified young lady, but she knows I love her to be a bit slangy now and then, just to show she's human. Our love grew out of a very fine friendship. At first we merely went around together as pals, she always encouraging and aiding me with sensible, calm, friendly advice. Then I took a trip to New York. Suddenly I found I was having an awfully slow time, though I know a lot of people. "What the deuce is the matter with me?" I asked myself. Suddenly I realised I was missing Alice. I called her up on the telephone right away. And from 3000 miles away — I asked her to marry me. Awfully unromantic, wasn't it? But Alice paid me back. She evaded me. "When are you coming back?" she asked. I said, "Well, I'll be on my way right now." And I did . . . But she won't marry me right away . . . She says, "Let's wait and be sure. It's better to change one's mind before than afterwards''.'

'I don't know how she puts up with me,' said Ingram with affectionate gallantry. 'I never take her to the theatre, nor do I care much for dancing. I'm absorbed in my work much of the time when other girls would, I am sure, think I should be with my fiancée. But she's always the same serene companion, genial, sympathetic and helpful. I've had many a valuable suggestion from her.'

First plans were that the marriage should take place after completion of *The Prisoner of Zenda*. There was a rumour that the pair would return to Ireland and be married by Rex's father. But Alice pooh-poohed this idea, jokingly

Rex and Alice at the time of her last film in 1929.

remarking that Rex would probably dump her with his relations, while he beat it across to Paris and the gay lights.

Eventually they went to South Pasadena to a little adobe house that took Rex's fancy. He just went in and asked if the people had any objection to his being married there. And there they were married on 5 November 1921. It was a Saturday. On Sunday they went to see three films — *Camille* with Nazimova and Valentino, *The Sheik* with Valentino, and a Mary Pickford film. On the Monday they were back at the studio for the filming of *The Prisoner of Zenda*. When the film was completed the young couple went for their honeymoon to San Francisco where they visited prisons and Chinatown with the mayor. Scarcely a conventional honeymoon. When Alice completed *Zenda* she did not appear in Rex's next film *Trifling Women*. However, it was not long before she was back at the studio again.

She was a most capable housewife. The Ingrams lived simply and avoided excitements and extravagances of Hollywood life. Rex was busy with his film projects and Alice did not allow her career to interfere with her domestic chores. While she enjoyed acting in films, she was not consumed with a burning ambition to get to the top and stay there at all costs. She was a happy person with simple tastes, accepting gratefully all that her new status brought her, but with feet firmly on the ground.

She had her own ideas and her own basic philosophy of life. Her views on her leading men were shrewd. She liked Valentino as a person, as he was very kind to her when working in the studio. His charm made every woman feel she was the only woman in the world. As an actor and lover of the screen, 'he always suggested more than he gave. He underacted always. I gave the effect of great passions under restraint. I always had the impression that I was playing with a volcano that might erupt at any minute. It never did, but that was the secret of his appeal. That was why women loved him. Curiosity? Well, maybe, but that's love in a sense. Isn't it?'

Her favourites were the Latins. Of the Anglo-Saxon race she had a poor opinion — 'I'd as soon have a chair as the typical man.' Novarro, whom she admired the most, had, she thought, the grace and restraint of Valentino and the vitality of Antonio Moreno, who for her came nearer to the simple, natural man than any of the others. He was physical, virile and active. Ivan Petrovitch personified the elemental lover — he conveyed a great strength free of crudeness. 'Ramon', she said, 'was the best actor of all. I think there was no picture that you could put him in that he couldn't have reached to every scene and I think the others could not have. I think that Valentino was so much a type that he couldn't have played certain scenes . . . Lewis Stone was another good actor. He played every scene well, but there was never any height to it. Tony Moreno was a good actor, but I couldn't have seen him in certain parts. Ramon, though, I could have seen in almost any part outside of an American boy. I think he had more ham in him — I don't like to use the word ham. Maybe it's nerve or confidence to get up and try something where someone like Ronald Colman, for instance, wouldn't try because he would feel silly. But Ramon would attempt anything — comedy, drama, crazy scenes, everything, and he could do it. I always thought he was capable of doing better than almost anyone except possibly John Barrymore who had the same thing.'

In her day Alice's own acting was regarded as 'adequate' — a damning expression. She was felt to be cold and reserved. But that was the time of much flamboyance of gesture and today as an actress Alice Terry looks simply restrained and moving in her conception of her role. It is the difference between Duse and Bernhardt. On the screen the inner spiritual performance of the one contrasts with the external mechanics of the other. I am thinking of *Cenere* and *Queen Elizabeth,* the two films of these famous actresses of the theatre. In fact one wonders today if the most impressive performance in *The Four Horsemen of the Apocalypse* is not given by Alice Terry. She would be the first to acknowledge her sympathetic response to Ingram's direction, but this should not minimise the real and charming talent she brought to the screen.

The statements of actors and actresses are not always worth recording but Alice's views on love should surely be repeated: 'While I do not claim to be an authority capable of offering advice to those in love or contemplating falling in love, I (naturally, like everyone else) have given it no little thought and have my own ideas about it.

'Love to me is a feeling of great tenderness, companionship and sincere respect for another. It is something which makes you want to be with the one you care for — which gives you a feeling of security and rest and peace.

'As a very young girl my idea of love was greatly exaggerated. I thought it was some great and turbulent sensation which would strike me like a cyclone and leave me dazed and trembling — that would send me reeling.

'However, now I· know that such a feeling could never be a lasting devotion and bring real happiness. This miscalled love can mean but misery and suffering.

'Real love, the kind that lasts and brings companionship and happiness to one's old age, must be founded on mutual respect and trust — a sort of glorified friendship — and is greatly helped along by similar tastes for people, pleasures, plays and books. Some of the finest love matches which I have seen among my married friends have begun as friendships and ripened into a truly beautiful love.

'Of one thing I am as positive as of Life and Death — without mutual trust and respect there can be no great and lasting love.'

These words were set down in print in 1924. The relationship between Alice and Rex must have been strained at times; there were long periods of separation. But when Rex lay dying in a Hollywood hospital twenty-six years later, Alice, his devoted wife and friend, was with him in his last moments of consciousness.

Ingram with his adopted son Kada-Abd-el-Kader.

TRIFLING WOMEN, *Metro 1922. Barbara La Marr and Ramon Novarro.*

8 Farewell to Hollywood

It was now the middle of 1922. Ingram undertook a remake of *Black Orchids* of 1916. He had two new players to groom, Ramon Novarro and Barbara La Marr. Both had played in *The Prisoner of Zenda* and were regarded as Ingram discoveries. Valentino had played in many films before Ingram had him under his control. Likewise with Novarro. Barbara La Marr had played Milady de Winter in Fairbank's *The Three Musketeers* (1921). But certainly it was Ingram who drew out the best and launched them on careers of some importance. He devoted much thought to building up their screen personalities and public image. In the case of Novarro he went all out to create another Valentino, and saw to it that Ramon had good publicity stills. Alice Terry pointed out that Novarro was getting all the attention while any old still of her was good enough!

Barbara La Marr was above all a screen vamp. Her acting ability was not of the highest, but her undoubted beauty made an impression on the screen. In *Trifling Women*, the remake of *Black Orchids*, she had a vehicle worthy of her particular talents. Her life story reads like the most lurid Hollywood fiction. Born on 28 July 1896 at North Yakima, Washington, according to what appears the most reliable version, she was kidnapped at fifteen, widowed at sixteen, and at seventeen found herself married to a bigamist. It was then she took up a career of dancing and vaudeville. She wrote six scenarios for the Fox Company which brought her $10,000. Douglas Fairbanks gave her a small part in *The Nut* (1921), and the Ingram films sealed her success. However, she was addicted to drugs, and died at Altadena, California in February 1926, shortly after making *The Girl From Montmartre*. During the four days of lying in state in Los Angeles 75,000 people passed the bier. She was buried in a mausoleum in Hollywood Cemetery.

People lost their heads over her. Edwin Schallert of the *Los Angeles Times* wrote: 'She is made for lurking tragedy . . . one feels the beat of raven's wings about her . . . she mirrors even joy as would a deep tarn . . . her radiance is that of moonlight in the heavy shadows of the night . . . Calypso she is, burning with a flame of subtle ecstasy.' This was the general journalistic approach to this diva.

The hectic plot of *Trifling Women (Black Orchids)* told, as we have already said, of a seductress who lures a father and son to their doom, causes the death by poisoning of an aged admirer and the death of her husband from duelling wounds. This gave Ingram the opportunity of creating feverish Gothic dreams, medieval castles and a claustrophobic world of poisoned passions. Attended by her pet ape and her dwarf companions, Zareda (Zoraida in the first version)

TRIFLING WOMEN, *Metro 1922.* Top:*The faithful companion.* Bottom: *Barbara La Marr as Zarenda with John George.*

was the ideal vamp. Into this film Ingram poured all his pictorial talent.

Robert Florey and Jean Count de Limur were engaged as advisors for the French atmosphere. The pictorial effects were very elaborate and extensive use was made of the matte shots developed by John Seitz. This trick effect creates illusions of magnificence by combining full-scale structures with miniatures and using masks on the lens. As it helps the cameraman to control what the camera sees and to select or eliminate elements to compose a new image, it has many applications and is a standard technique of modern film-making. It was first introduced by Seitz in *Trifling Women* and patented by him later in 1928. The castle was created by hanging foreground miniatures and using a black surround combined with a life-size tower. The miniatures were made by Griffith's cameraman, G. Billy Bitzer. All the telephone poles and fences on the Metro lot were matted out for the film. By double exposure, done in the camera, clouds were introduced into the shots of the castle. The bizarre and evocative settings were by Leo Kuter.

The matte technique was used too, to get over an unusual problem that arose during production. Barbara La Marr was always accompanied in the film by a great chimpanzee named Joe Martin. The creature became very attached to Barbara and became very aggressive to strangers. Edward Connelly had occasion to attempt to put a necklace around her neck which later in the film she was to take off and put around the monkey's neck. Joe thought Connelly was attacking Barbara and he went for him and held him so tight that blood came from his fingernails. The terrified Connelly was extracted from the animal's clutches and refused point blank to appear in any further scenes with Joe. By a clever use of the matte technique, the scenes of the two together were completed without their meeting. The keeper of the animal was later dismissed for cruelty and met an appropriate end when he was trampled to death by a circus elephant.

Ingram himself took his new protégés through their paces. According to Novarro, in an interview I had with him, he was a hard taskmaster, but he did illuminate the characters for them to ensure a final result gratifying to both director and actor. In *Zenda,* he had Novarro practise throwing his monocle in the air and catching it in his eye. On another occasion Novarro was reduced to cold fury when he spent an afternoon rehearsing with Barbara La Marr the gentle art of being slapped across the face.

Trifling Women had its New York première at the Astor Theatre on 2 October 1922. It had a good press. The *New York Times* spoke of the fascinating imagery with which Ingram filled his screen, and of the compulsive effect of those pictures which haunted him. They called it 'an old tale made fascinating by telling'. The *Moving Picture World* wrote: 'Mr Ingram's direction of this production is superb and practically faultless. The story moves at a deliberate tempo which allows the full force of every scene and act to be impressed on the spectator and the film holds your undivided attention throughout. It is from every standpoint an impressive production, handsomely mounted, pictorially striking, with many weird effects, as for instance where the young lover's father dies from drinking poison he intended for another, and the scene closes with the old roué still seated at the banquet table with a chimpanzee drinking a toast to him. Artistically the production is an achievement . . .'

Lewis Stone and Edward Connelly, both seasoned players, gave of their best. Novarro added to his laurels and Barbara La Marr carried her characterisation of the *femme fatale* to operatic dimensions.

Nicholas Schenck who was to become President of MGM on the death of Marcus Loew preferred *Trifling Women* to *The Four Horsemen*. Being the curious personal film it was, it did not make much impact on the public. Today the stills suggest that it might be interesting to see. It is one of those forgotten films of which one hopes a copy will appear some day.

In the mid-twenties Hollywood was undergoing a real estate boom and involved itself more with big business than movies. Ingram was becoming tired of the place. Although he had *carte blanche* at Metro, he noted tendencies to take control away from the individual director and place it in the hands of studio executives and front-office men. His criticisms of Hollywood made him enemies in powerful quarters. For some time he had considered making films abroad. The reasons are complex. He had observed European film developments and admired the best work coming from the studios of Germany and France. Moreover, he was after all a European and wanted a new challenge. He had decided views on the relationship of a film story to its natural background. In his films he tried to develop a fidelity to story environment which he achieved through much research and reading. His meticulous realism demanded that the players even speak the language of the country represented. Three of his main films for Metro had been set in France. His health had never been robust and he may have needed a change of climate. It was rumoured that

Above: **TRIFLING WOMEN,** *Metro 1922. Ingram directs. Edward Connelly, Hughie Mack and Lewis Stone.*

he wished to retire from films and devote himself to his abiding passion, sculpture. Ultimately he announced that he wished to make films abroad — a decision that caused some antagonism from local Hollywood patriots.

His next film was based on a South Sea island story by John Russell — *The Passion Vine*. It came to the screen as *Where the Pavement Ends,* the title of the book from which the story was taken. This, at least, got him away from Hollywood, as it was shot on location. The first part of the film was made in Florida where the studio built by Glen Curtis, the airman, at Hialeah was used. Set-building delayed shooting for a month at Hialeah. Much improvisation was necessary — for one lighting effect thirty-two mirrors were borrowed from the local hotel. There were no storms in Florida at the time, so for the waterfall sequences which formed such an important part of the story the company moved to Cuba. Great structures had to be built by Gordon Mayer, a local architect for the overhead shots of the forests.

Mike Fitzgerald, an Irish find of Ingram, was 'grip' to Seitz. The employment of Gordon Avil as another assistant was providential as he rescued Alice Terry from drowning in the torrent at the waterfall during production. Whytock mentions that Ingram did not go on to Cuba as he was not feeling well. His assistant in charge of production was Colonel Starrett Ford, John Russell, the author, also joined the unit on location. Some of the scenes are supposed to have been shot in the New York Studios. Ingram hoped to have Maurice Costello in the film: 'I wanted Maurice Costello to play the old captain in this picture, but it was the villain's role and Costello would have everybody liking him better than they did the hero. He couldn't help it. That's the way I'd feel about him. He's one of the screen's greatest actors — I wish I could do a picture that would bring him back as he ought to come.' Another old actor from Vitagraph, Harry Morey, got the role. Alice Terry returned to the screen in the role of Matilda Spener, the missionary's daughter who develops a tragic love for a native boy, played by Ramon Novarro. Among the cast was Rosita Ramírez, a child player who was a grand-daughter of a former president of Cuba. She subsequently acted in many Ingram films and as Rosita Garcia was his leading lady in his last film.

At the beginning of September Ingram travelled east with Colonel Starrett Ford and Alice. He mapped out the script on the train, only interrupting his journey to visit his friends Robert Z. Leonard and his wife, Mae Murray, at their home at Great Neck, Long Island.

Ingram's films were not noted for their happy endings, but for this film he made two endings, one happy and the other, which he preferred, tragic.

While he was working on *Where the Pavement Ends* he received news that *Ben Hur* was going to be made without him. This was a pet project of his and he had it written into his contract that, should the film be made by another company than Metro, he would be released to make it. The severe blow of the loss of this assignment led to a definite change in his personality which was noticed by his friends. Other directors who wanted to make this film were D. W. Griffith and Erich von Stroheim.

On completion of *Where the Pavement Ends* Rex returned to New York to consult with Marcus Loew. The film had its première at the Capitol Theatre, New York on 1 April 1923. In *The Best Moving Pictures of 1922-23* Robert

WHERE THE PAVEMENT ENDS, *Metro 1923. Alice Terry and Ramon Novarro.*

WHERE THE PAVEMENT ENDS, *Metro 1923. Rex and Alice on location.*

Emmet Sherwood, a devoted admirer of Ingram, gave it honourable mention: 'The glamorous romance and hopeless tragedy of the South Sea Islands were reproduced by Rex Ingram in *Where the Pavement Ends*. He made the picture reflect both these qualities and did it in a legitimate way. *Where the Pavement Ends* was too long for its substance — it exhausted several reels before it even scratched the surface of drama — but it was gorgeously beautiful and it was dignified by intelligence and sincerity in its treatment.'

The film was chosen to open the new Tivoli Theatre, London, on 6 September 1923. This was once a variety theatre and the stage show for the opening included Marie Dainton in an impersonation of the famous Marie Lloyd, Little Tich himself, and Mr Malcolm Scott. Madame Kirby Lunn sang the National Anthem. G. A. Atkinson didn't like the film, but Michael Orme in *The Sketch* thought: 'more exciting than *Way Down East*, more poetic than *Prisoner of Zenda*, it is a film that was worthy of the occasion (the opening of the Tivoli Cinema). In a market of mediocrity it towers above them all and lifts the screen to its rightful place . . . the film captures the Russell story in a remarkable way.'

The next assignment, a congenial one for Ingram, resulted in one of his more attractive and popular films. *Scaramouche*, by Rafael Sabatini, was a highly successful novel about the French Revolution. In Willis Goldbeck, Ingram

SCARAMOUCHE, *Metro 1923. The duel.*

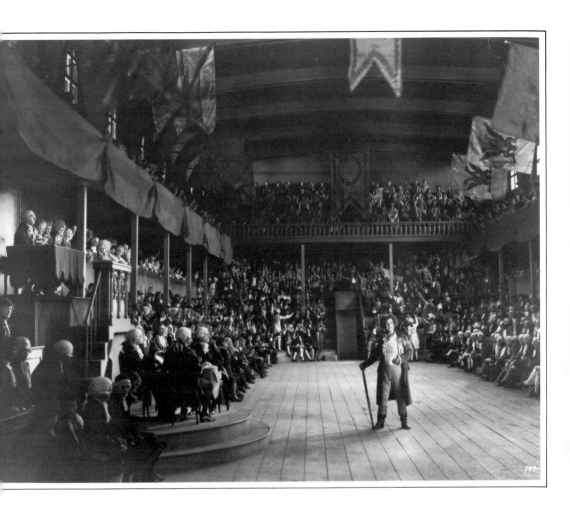

SCARAMOUCHE, *Metro 1923. Danton addresses the Assembly.*

Overleaf: SCARAMOUCHE, *The massacre of the Swiss Guard.*

found an ideal scriptwriter. The Terry-Novarro team was continued and Lewis Stone was chosen to play the villain. Amongst the carefully selected cast were William Humphrey, Rex's old director from Vitagraph, as well as the Vitagraph actress Julia Swayne Gordon. Otto Matieson, a new arrival from Denmark, played the hero's ecclesiastical student friend; George Siegman played Danton; de Garcia Fuerberg was Robespierre; and the relatively small role of Napoleon was taken by Slavko Vorkapich, a young Slav actor who later became MGM's expert on montage and who is best remembered for his earthquake sequence in *San Francisco* of 1936. Jacques Tourneur, later to become an important director, being then a young student played in the crowd scenes. This was his film debut.

The production began on 17 March 1923, St Patrick's Day. It would continue for four to five months. According to Seitz, there was no shooting for twelve days after Patrick's Day as Rex was still celebrating. This sounds more like legend than fact. Elaborate sets were built and a complete French village was constructed in the San Fernando Valley, the other sets being erected on the Metro lot. Fifteen hundred extras were used. Much research had gone into the project and Ingram had even been able to borrow the original rosette worn by Danton on the scaffold, a tiny detail that only he would have concerned himself with.

As ever Ingram carried through production with his usual flair for eccentricity. When the mob stormed through the streets of Paris on their way to the Tuileries he had the studio orchestra (which was always standing by to provide atmosphere for the players) strike up *The Wearing of the Green* and other Irish patriotic songs. His selection of types for the film was impressive. Amongst the extras was a half-crazed character known as Holy Mary, whose avowed intention was to convert Ingram to Catholicism.

Curt Rehfeld, an assistant, helped Ingram to manoeuvre his crowds with intelligence, achieving effects which surpassed those of the master, D. W. Griffith. Rehfeld had army experience and was responsible for extras and their equipment. He inaugurated a system of punched tickets and extras didn't get paid until they returned props and costumes. Turnstiles were set up so that extras could be accurately checked. Rehfeld's wooden leg caused him to fall from his horse at one point during the production.

One of the visitors to the set was Victor Sjöström, the great Swedish pioneer who later directed the first film for the future MGM company.

Sabatini's story had all the elements of popular success: the story of star-crossed lovers set against the tragic story of Marie Antoinette, the colourful settings of the Revolution, duels, strolling players, tyrannical aristocrats and suffering peasants, and locations ranging from Brittany to Paris.

On 15 September 1923 the film was presented, under the auspices of the Red Cross, in aid of Japanese relief at the Belasco Theatre, Washington. Ingram was present and thanked the audience for their enthusiastic reception of his film. On 30 September the New York première was held at the 44th Street Theatre and again Ingram received a tremendous ovation for another great success.

Although Novarro and Alice Terry gave formidable performances, it was Lewis Stone's film. His study of the cynical marquis seemed to embody the

SCARAMOUCHE, *Metro 1923. Alice Terry and Lewis Stone.*

inhumanity of a whole generation of eighteenth-century aristocrats. His was a perfect performance. The visual beauty of the production and the exquisite photography of John Seitz made it quite an exciting film to watch. Forty-three years after, Kevin Brownlow, an experienced technician and film director of *It Happened Here,* saw the film at George Eastman House, Rochester, NY. He gives an interesting retrospective view: '*Scaramouche* is primarily a work of art in the 18th century tradition. The period has been so beautifully evoked that it seems inconceivable that the picture belongs to this century. It looks as though the combined efforts of several 18th century painters, sculptors, scenic designers, costumiers and architects have reached a climax of rococo glory on celluloid. Ingram's classically ascetic style bears little relation to the self-indulgence of the man himself. It bears little relation to the style of any other director. It shows considerable artistic progress from the already promising *Four Horsemen* . . . The narrative is swiftly flowing but is nevertheless an undercurrent. *Scaramouche* clearly attracted Ingram for its visual qualities rather than for its thrilling story. Characterisations remain within the formal detached pattern. One could easily dismiss Ingram's contribution, and lay the credit for the artistic success of *Scaramouche* at the feet of John Seitz. His work deserves a richer description than that of mere 'photography' for it achieves a standard of interpretation few cameramen could even understand,

SCARAMOUCHE, *Metro 1923. Ingram directs Novarro while Victor Sjöström (second figure below Ingram) looks on.*

let alone duplicate. Seitz was chosen by Ingram, he was not a studio assignment. They worked together as a team, and they understood each other's requirements. A successful motion picture requires more than a good director; the chemistry must be right — the elements of cameraman, scenarist, art director, and producer must contribute to the end result in exactly the right degree. Whatever the problems of production *Scaramouche* succeeded because the fusion of creative talents was perfect. It is tragic that the formula should have been lost.

'Von Sternberg considered *Scaramouche* to be Ingram's best film, and it is easy to see why it should appeal to him. The carefully chosen faces, from a pock-marked wine-bloated face of an aristocrat to the porcelain-china beauty of Alice Terry, play as important a part in the creation of atmosphere as the authentic costumes and the remarkable lavish sets. The art-director has not merely supplied the buildings; under Ingram's fanatically sharp eye he has added tangles of overhead washing lines, battered wooden drainpipes and guttering, open sewers, over which ladies have to be carried, and, above all, *height,* that rarest of qualities in American Art Direction, which too often assumes that the audience must see everything especially the roof, and therefore constructs buildings to the proportions of the screen . . .

'The performances are academically beautiful rather than warm and human.

SCARAMOUCHE, *Metro 1923. Garcia Fuerburg as Robespierre.*

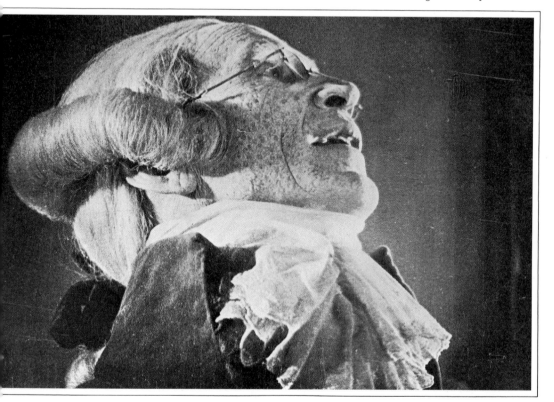

In such a classical piece, however, this is a virtue rather than a fault. Novarro is excellent within this formal category; in some scenes he is electrifying. One doesn't care for these characters, one just watches them with complete aesthetic satisfaction . . . *Scaramouche* for the Cinema is an old master.'

It was announced in January 1925 that *Scaramouche* had helped to win the Zukor award of $10,000 for its writer, Rafael Sabatini, whose story had made the best movie in the year ended 1 September 1924. His other stories *Captain Blood, The Sea Hawk* and *Bardelys the Magnificent* also provided excellent material for films. It may be noted that John McCormack, the Irish tenor, studied under his father in Italy.

The selection panel included Charles Dana Gibson, Allan Dwan, Mary Roberts Reinhart, Elmer Rice, and Robert E. Sherwood. It made its choice from films as distinguished as Chaplin's *Woman of Paris*, Raoul Walsh's *Thief of Bagdad*, de Mille's *Ten Commandments*, John Griffith Wray's *Anna Christie* and Sidney Olcott's *Monsieur Beaucaire*.

The citation for the prize reads as follows: '*Scaramouche*, from all view-points, was an exceptional motion picture. It possessed that fluidity of action which is essential to effectiveness on the screen; it reflected realistically a particularly dramatic period of history — the period of the French Revolution; it possessed a great pictorial beauty in costumes, backgrounds and the composition of scenes; it was directed with skill and appreciation by Mr Ingram, and played by a brilliant cast; above all it was a good story — founded on the basic principles of drama and embellished with striking detail. The credit for this is Mr Sabatini's. He wrote *Scaramouche* with consistent attention to the continuity of his narrative and regard for the eloquence of the dramatic incident. The strokes of his pen were broad — his mood heroic. For that reason *Scaramouche* provided ideal material for a motion picture. Mr Goldbeck the adaptor could mould it into the necessary scenario form without sacrificing the vigor, the flavour or the sense of the original.'

As we have seen, Ingram had longed for the day he could get away from Hollywood, its coteries, gossip, and inevitable scramble for power, increasing bureaucracy and production controls. As Grant Whytock put it: 'The big problem with Hollywood today is they're shooting schedules, they're not shooting pictures. With Rex Ingram's films they didn't see how much they were going to cost, they used to figure out how much they were going to make. They agreed on a round figure — like *Scaramouche*, I think we budgeted for thirteen weeks and it went seventeen.' Eventually Ingram got a grudging permission to make *The Arab* on natural locations in Tunisia, the interiors to be shot in Paris in a studio near Joinville.

Before this, however, Rex and Alice had taken a trip to London where they met his father. In Ireland the guerilla warfare against Britain was turned against local supporters of the hereditary enemy. Pro-British people suspected of giving support to the Crown forces were summarily shot and houses of people with pro-British leanings were destroyed. As a pro-British sympathiser with a son in the British army, the Reverend Mr Hitchcock found himself an enemy alien in a country where he had lived all his life. An old order was changing and the Ireland of his particular class was to be the loser. Entries in his preacher's book indicate the tragic events and feelings of the time: 'May 19th 1920. Mr Andrew

Armstrong's brother was wounded seriously by Sinn Feiners at Phibsboro — shot in the back as usual. May 15th 1921. Tuesday — two policemen killed in ambush in the village by Sinn Feiners . . .. May 22nd 1921. Great military activity in Kinnitty . . . July 3rd 1921. Two Pearsons of Coolacrease shot dead and house burnt.'

After the forced treaty of 1921, a tragic civil war broke out between those who supported the new Irish Free State and those who regarded it as a betrayal of republican principles. Another entry in his preacher's book reads: 'Good Friday 1922. Siege of Kinnitty. Free Staters in the office and Republican Forces all round. Both forces evacuated the village in the night by agreement. Only one shot fired. Settlement brought about largely through the Rector, Dr Hitchcock, who went backwards and forwards between both forces and paved the way for peace.'

Dr Hitchcock left Ireland hurriedly in the beginning of 1924 to become rector at Tolleshunt Knights, Essex. He was a man of brilliant attainments, but too aggressive and tactless to be appointed a bishop. He could be tenaciously obstinate and in 1918 he took an ecclesiastical action against the Protestant Primate of Ireland, the Most Reverend John Baptist Crozier, D.D. He lost the case and with it his chances of promotion. He had to be content with an honorary doctorate of literature conferred on him by his old Alma Mater, Trinity College. His son inherited his litigious qualities.

The meeting of the father and the son must have been a moving one. The more their differences, the more alike they were, for the arrogance was there in both. The aggressive Christian must, however, have felt perturbed by the free-thinking hedonist his son had become.

The rest of Rex's time in Europe was spent looking around, making acquaintances and noting facilities for production. The prospects were pleasing and he was elated by the success he had achieved. He found more congenial company than Hollywood could provide, but he made the fatal mistake of giving an interview to the French papers in which he said that he was so pleased with Europe that he could never make another film in Hollywood. This proved to be prophetic and the article, when read in Hollywood by colleagues who were then preparing equipment for transport abroad, filled them with foreboding. It was also being noted down for future reference by two of Hollywood's elite publicists — Miss Louella Parsons and Mr James R. Quirk, editor of *Photoplay*.

Ingram duly reached Tunisia and shot his scenes for *The Arab,* mostly in the south of the country at Gabes and Sidi Bou Said. A good horseman, he enjoyed competing with the Arab riders and took part in one of the spectacular scenes of the film. He felt a strange affinity with the Arab people, approving of their rather passive attitude to life, contrasting it with the rush and bustle of American habits. Undoubtedly, he was beginning to react against the tense hard-working life he had been leading in Hollywood. He found the relaxed atmosphere more agreeable. He made many influential friends in Tunis including the Bey who conferred the Order of Niftkan Itchkar on him as well as presenting him with his personal court jester, Shorty Ben Mairech, who remained with Rex for many years. He and Alice adopted the Arab boy Abd-el-Kader who played in several of the films.

Back in Paris for the interiors, there were the usual problems of make-

158-316

shift production. Jean de Limur tells an amusing story of the arrival of an imported snake-charmer with her pets in two hat-boxes. A room for the lady having been found after some difficulty, she went off one day leaving her precious charges behind in the hotel. On her return she found that they had escaped from their boxes. One had climbed up the curtains and was eating them. The other was creating havoc on the mantlepiece with its tail. The floor and furniture were strewn with bric-a-brac. Not even the wallpaper had escaped.

At this time Ingram met Harry Lachman, a photographer and painter whose work had been hung in the Luxembourg Palace. Lachman was to become much involved in Ingram's Nice studio project. Rex had been impressed with Nice as a centre for film production. It is conveniently situated on the Mediterranean, within easy reach of Spain, Italy and North Africa. As well as a varied scenery of hills and sea, and a good climate, it had a tradition of film-making which went back to the good old days of Jean Durand and his comedies. It had provided settings for many films of importance. That very year, 1925, while Ingram was surveying its possibilities and taking the first shots for *Mare Nostrum,* the great Louis Feuillade, maker of the serials *Judex, Fantomas* and *The Vampires,* died there.

The Arab was a formula picture, designed to display Novarro in a romantic

Below: THE ARAB, *Metro-Goldwyn 1924. Ingram, Alice Terry and Ramon Novarro.*
Previous page: THE ARAB, *Jamil leads the Christian children to safety.*

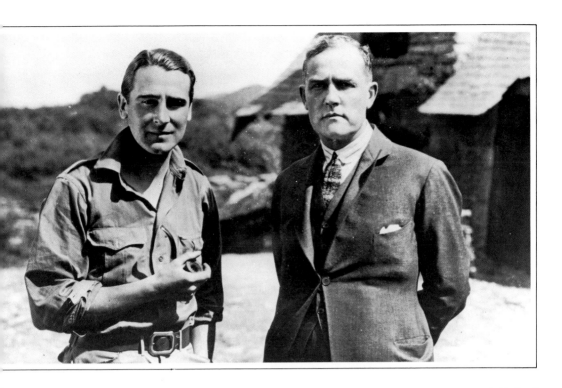

Top: *Rex Ingram with Victor Sjöström, master of the Swedish cinema who was to direct the first MGM film and to play the role of the Professor in Bergman's* WILD STRAWBERRIES. Bottom: *Friend and Foe. Marcus Loew (left) and Louis B Mayer.*

THE ARAB, *Metro-Goldwyn 1924. Ramon Novarro and Alice Terry.*

role to compete with Valentino in *The Sheik.* The story was based on the Edgar Selwyn play, which had been filmed previously by Lasky with Selwyn himself in the lead. The story dealt with a missionary's daughter in love with an Arab chief's son and of the machinations of an unscrupulous governor who plans a massacre of the Christians.

The story is weak and the characterisations not particularly good. Novarro is pleasantly presented, but the lack of continuity suggests improvisation of the script as the unit went from location to location. Ingram himself does some fool-acting not very much in keeping with the plot. Maxudian as the governor has a fine presence and survives the general failure to co-ordinate story and settings, the latter being very beautiful at times. When John Seitz shot scenes of camels in the sunset in January 1924 he was almost frozen to death. Used in the film were 800 camels and 400 horses. The contact man was Chief of Police and was an Italian Arab. It was given its New York première on 13 July 1924. The film was presented in London to celebrate the first anniversary of the Tivoli Theatre, which had opened the previous year with another Ingram film.

While Ingram was away, a merger took place between the Metro and Goldwyn Companies on 17 April 1924. Loew's, Inc. invited Louis B. Mayer and his associates, Irving Thalberg and J. Robert Rubin, to come into the new organisation, with Mayer as Vice-President and General Manager. Culver City, the old studio of Thomas Ince who had died that year, was to be the new West-

Coast headquarters. Metro-Goldwyn Pictures was to be the new title, but Mayer-controlled productions were to be known as a Louis B. Mayer production for Metro-Goldwyn, or a Metro-Goldwyn-Mayer Production. The last title became permanent. Mayer had a three-year contract with the company and soon began to develop the power of an oriental despot. He was most unpopular with the independent-minded old guard of directors, including Marshall Neilan, von Stroheim and Ingram. Ingram who loathed him had written into his contract that his films should be simply known as Rex Ingram Productions for Metro-Goldwyn, without mention of Mayer. When Mayer took over Culver City on 17 May 1924 there were many absentees at his party. The prodigal children were waiting to get out or be pushed out. The first MGM film was to be the striking *He Who Gets Slapped* made by Victor Sjöström with Lon Chaney, John Gilbert and Norma Shearer.

Ingram was able to detach himself as much as possible from Mayer and report only to Marcus Loew and Nicholas Schenck in New York. The scene was now set for his departure to Europe and the Nice studios. His sponsors realised his fixed purpose and gave way.

Before we take leave of him on the eve of departure there is one more story to be told. *Ben Hur* had always been a desirable property and the play had been jealously guarded by Abe Erlanger. When Kalem made a film version in 1907 a huge lawsuit resulted which defined the position of film copyright for the first time. Douglas Fairbanks wanted the story from Klaw and Erlanger, but it was clear that it was going to be expensive. The screen rights became vested in a specially-formed organisation called Classical Cinematograph Corporation, and from these Joe Godsol of the Goldwyn Company acquired it for half the financial returns on the film — certainly an unusual contract. June Mathis persuaded Erlanger to have her in charge of production. This may explain why Ingram was not given the direction as there was little love between the pair by this time. Charles Brabin, a former director of Ingram at Edison and the husband of Theda Bara, got the job. George Walsh was to play the lead. Major Ed. Bowes was to supervise and the role of Messala was to go to the veteran Francis X. Bushman. It is interesting to note that one of the most famous stage Messalas was William S. Hart, the famous cowboy star. Bowes and Brabin went to Rome in August 1923 to make a preliminary survey. June Mathis and George Walsh followed six months later and the players were assembled. Mussolini had promised to provide facilities. In due course some sea scenes were filmed at Anzio, but it was becoming clear that all was not well with production. In the meantime the merger had taken place, and Mayer, who decided to go on with the film, set out for Italy with some friends. It must be put on record that he invited Ingram to take over the production, but Ingram made so many conditions that Mayer refused to consider them. The upshot of the matter was that Fred Niblo replaced Brabin, Ramon Novarro replaced George Walsh and even June Mathis had to give way to Bess Meredyth. The Italian scenes were scrapped. In January 1925 the company was ordered home and shooting continued at Culver City including the great chariot race scene. Shooting time was eighteen months and the film ran to twelve reels, three hours by silent standards. It had its world première at the George M. Cohan Theatre in New York on 30 December 1925. Originally budgeted at $750,000, it finally cost $4 million. The net earnings were $6 million. The rest is film history. But it was not the end of the film for Ingram since he was later to profit materially by its Italian disaster.

THE ARAB, *Metro-Goldwyn 1924. Ramon Novarro and Alice Terry.*

9 Projects and Opinions

Ingram was a romantic figure, as handsome as any of his leading men and, moreover, married to the beautiful Alice Terry. He was always good for an article in the fan magazines and all that concerned this fascinating pair got full coverage. He was communicative about his views on the cinema and was an eloquent propagandist for its artistic claims. He believed strongly that a film gained enormously if it was shot on the actual location of the story. This was nothing new. As early as 1911 Sidney Olcott of the Kalem Company took a group of players to Killarney, Palestine and Egypt to make films appropriate to those locations. Similarly, Robert Flaherty in 1920 pioneered story actuality in Greenland and the South Seas, thereby making film history. Ingram supported his theory against all the opposition of Hollywood whose producers felt more at home in the hot-house atmosphere of studio construction. Things have changed now and today we may note the almost complete reliance of television series and a great number of Hollywood movies on location shooting.

Ingram had always paid the greatest attention to authentic backgrounds in his films. This was something he shared with his friend von Stroheim. In *The Four Horsemen of the Apocalypse* the feeling of wartime France is meticulously captured just as von Stroheim captured the essence of Monte Carlo in *Foolish Wives.*

D. W. Griffith was regarded as the great sentimentalist of the cinema, von Stroheim as its realist and Ingram as the romantic. But Ingram had no small element of realism in his work. Von Stroheim as reported in the *New York Times* of 5 August 1923 said: 'Little realism has been seen on the screen. There are *Miss Lulu Bett* (by William de Mille), some of the Will Rogers pictures, *Grandma's Boy* (Harold Lloyd) and *The Kid* in comedies. Certain moments in Marshall Neilan's pictures have possessed the spark, as did the two-reel production of O'Henry's *The Cop and the Anthem* and other O'Henry stories. There was realism in Rex Ingram's *The Conquering Power* and that to my mind is about all. There must be more realism on the screen, and it is my humble ambition to furnish some of it. It is with that idea that I am working hard on Norris's *McTeague,* which will be introduced to the screen under the title of *Greed* and I have other works in mind that I hope to produce.'

Ingram's position with his company was supreme. His name on a production was as much 'box-office' as that of a star, and his films made money. Ingram was not the man to compromise with the new bureaucratic controls of film-making. He was arrogant, with no respect whatsoever for authority. Nor was he exactly easy to get on with. He was an individualist to the point of eccentricity. His enemies granted him charm of manner, but he had a capacity for

Ingram (second from left) and John Ford (extreme right).

making enemies. He saw people in terms of black and white. He was generous to friends but, once crossed, the offender was cast into outer darkness. He let people know what he thought of them to their faces. He was his own pace-setter and took directions from nobody. He disliked social contacts but could, when the occasion demanded, appear at social functions, but he had a capacity for withdrawal which made some of his acquaintances believe that he never liked anybody. There was also a sense of frustration perceptible in the man as if there was some goal he was seeking which constantly eluded him. People who knew him are sharply divided into those who adored him and those who disliked him intensely.

When he gave interviews he let his imagination run away with him, and it is difficult to separate fact from fiction. Why? Partly, I think, because he had the Irishman's desire to please and amuse his listeners at all costs. He was very consciously Irish. He always tried to help a fellow-countryman. Although he never returned to Ireland he was tied to it by that same umbilical cord which never allowed James Joyce to escape from his early environment.

Amongst Irish Americans St Patrick's Day is an occasion of sentiment and Rex and Alice attended the St Patrick's Day celebrations of 1922 at the Ambassador Hotel, Los Angeles, where the dynamic P. A. Powers of the Robertson Cole Corporation presided as host. Inevitably the programme included renderings of *Mother Machree, Where the River Shannon Flows* and *My Wild Irish Rose.* Amongst the guests were the Japanese actor Sessue Hayakawa and his wife Tsuru Aoki and the delightful Bessie Love.

The departure from Hollywood was a major event in Ingram's life. Hitherto that life had been confined. An Irish village, New York and Hollywood represented his contact with the world. He had no knowledge of Europe, let alone Africa. But he had his father's capacity for scholarship and reading. Deep personal research went into each of his films and the French feeling emerges in *The Four Horsemen, The Conquering Power* and *Trifling Women.* Though he had never been to France, he worked closely with French consultants like Jean de Limur and Robert Florey.

With the production of *The Arab,* of course, Ingram made direct contact with North African life and became so steeped in its traditions and customs that it was to play a big part in his outlook for the coming years.

While in London in October 1923 he was given a lunch at the Savoy Hotel by the management of the Tivoli Cinema. G. H. Roberts, MP, was in the chair and his wife and father were present. I quote from the *Motion Picture Studio* of 20 October 1923:

Rex Ingram said that from a technical point of view a stage of near per-fection had been reached. But there was something lacking that made him realise that without change of environment, he had already given the best that was in him. America was a great country, but for the artist it was still too new. Atmosphere, colour and romance were missing, and nothing could replace them. They could only be found in older countries. It seemed to him, moreover, that American film production was entirely dominated by the supposed wants of the public and the reaction at the box-office. The instant a new type of film was successful, every producer in the country began to make slavish copies of it, which were usually far inferior to the model and fell flat. Titles for similar reasons were frequently changed, and films were thus sent into the world handicapped by the most ludicrously inappropriate names. As for him, he believed that the box-office should be the artist's last consideration, since it had been proved over and over again that it was quite impossible to say in advance what the public wanted. An artist should work to please himself, and if he was sincere he was sure to win the appreciation he deserved. Far too many films were produced, for only about one in every hundred was worth looking at. Among all the films he had seen he could recall no more than six which had made any lasting impression on him. So far as he was concerned, he felt that if he succeeded in making one film in a year he had done great work. He was convinced that there was a great future for British Film Production. Since he had been in London he had seen a new film *Woman to Woman* which, in his opinion, was the best yet produced anywhere.

Not exactly a statement to bring joy to the heart of Hollywood! In fact it would be difficult to conceive a more undiplomatic statement by a successful Hollywood director.

But Ingram poured out his views on every aspect of his work. In *Photoplay Research Society* of 1922 he wrote an article 'Directing the Picture: Opportunities in the Motion Picture Industry' in which he dealt with the growth of the cinema from its early days and its establishment as an art. He shows the influence of the arts of painting, sculpture, and drama on the people, but suggests that the influence of the cinema is greater. He deals with his own transition from sculpture to cinema and shows how the principles of one art can apply to another. He concludes with the words:

> What do you think the producers look for in a man when they engage him to take charge of one of their producing units? What qualifications are considered necessary in a successful director? May I tell you?
>
> 'First I should say, the ability to create. A broad acquaintance with the world at large; an intimate knowledge of the races; an understanding of how people live in the countries throughout the earth; and the power to visualise the written word in picture form.
>
> You sigh and say to yourself, 'This is indeed a hard profession to break into!' But I ask you is it? Would it not be equally as hard for one to break into your own profession whatever it may be, unless one had the training for it? Of course it would. If it were an easy thing to become a motion picture director, the studios would be full of them. It is because it is not an easy thing to become a director, that the work is so attractive. To those unfitted for it, there is no use allowing this work to make an appeal.
>
> The potential director had better be certain that he is a close student of human nature. To make this work stand out and achieve success, it is necessary that the characters he portrays on the screen appear as actual living, breathing persons. One of the surest ways to study human nature at first hand is to mix with all classes of people in all walks of life. Once you

are able to do this, you will come to know life, and be able to depict it humanly on the screen.

The director should also be a lover of books, and a natural tendency to analyse different dramatic situations will help immeasurably when you are finally qualified to handle the megaphone.

There is no sure road to the position of director for a motion picture producing company. Some of the rank and file of men and women now directing stars of the screen drifted quite naturally from the legitimate theatre into studio work. Others have served long apprenticeships as actors, writers and cameramen before they were qualified to direct a motion picture.

To know the camera is to know what is possible of it. Therefore a good many of our present-day directors have graduated from the ranks of cameraman. First of all they have the knowledge of the limitations or possibilities of the camera. Then they have gained a vast store of information by observing the methods of the various directors when they have served as cameramen.

Since the players are as clay in the hands of the sculptor, as paint at the tip of the artist's brush, it is desirable that, like the artist, the director should have a true sense of art values. He moulds them into the forms desired and called for by the author's script, in one instance, or he places and blends them on his canvas to conform with the story told by the author in another.'

In an article in *Photoplay Magazine* for June 1923 he spoke of his directing methods:

I once worked for a director who was gifted with a faculty for irritating everyone and not a thing did he get out of me. There was an aloof inhospitable atmosphere about the set. Assistants whispered, carpenters glowered and the great man himself made me feel that I was the worst specimen of an actor he had ever seen, and I certainly lived up to his expectations in that picture. Later I worked with a human, sympathetic director who gave me credit for having as much idea of my part as he had, and I think I lived up to his expectations too.

How far a little encouragement goes in any sort of work!

After my first day in the studio I resolved to be a director. My second resolution made soon afterwards was to be a human being — although a director. The first law I made for myself was: 'Make them Happy'. This is my golden rule with players old and new. I admit I break it every once in a while when the sun is going down and I want to finish the work with five hundred people. Every rule has its proving exception. To all players, particularly beginners, I want to cry 'Relax!' But you cannot make them relax by shouting at them. On the contrary they would immediately become tense and when an actor is tense he is not thinking normally. His imagination is benumbed.'

If there is one characteristic of Ingram's films it is the all-pervading atmosphere he manages to evoke and he is quoted on this subject by Peter Milne in his book *Motion Picture Directing* (New York, 1922):

After sincerity of characterisation and directness in story telling, atmosphere does more towards making an audience accept what it sees on the screen than anything else. By accept I mean be entertained, engrossed in the subject.

While good atmosphere gives an air of reality to a picture yet the most convincing and engrossing atmosphere is often far from realistic. This is so because the aim of the director should be to get over the effect of the atmosphere he desires, rather than the actual atmosphere which exists in such scenes as he may wish to portray, and which, if reduced literally to the screen, would be quite unconvincing . . .

Whether a scene is being made of a beach-comber's shanty, an underworld basement saloon, a pool-hall, a ship's cabin, a shoe factory or a smart restaurant, not only should the aim be to convince the audience, but enough study should be given to the subjects in each case, to convince the habitués of any of these places that they are in familiar surroundings.

One of the most interesting sets that I have ever handled from an atmospheric stand-point was the interior of a derelict ship, beached, and become the hangout of beach-combers, in *Under Crimson Skies,* a production some years old. Conrad, the master writer of the sea, never offered a more wonderful opportunity for colour than did this episode in the story provided by J. G. Hawks, with its thrilling climax in the battle in the surf between the white man and the black giant.

In *The Four Horsemen* the basement resort of the Buenos Aires *bocca* or riverside hangout, furnished plenty of chances to make colourful pictures — yet had I been literal in the way I handled it, the effect would not have been anything as nearly realistic. For I doubt if anything just like that dive ever existed in the Argentine or anywhere else for that matter.

The set was a Spanish version of a bowery cellar saloon that I used in a picture which I made several years before and re-created to suit the episodes suggested in the Blasco Ibáñez novel. The signs on the wall, the types of men, in fact all the bits of atmosphere in the place were the results of painstaking efforts to get 'colour' and local atmosphere into the set. In one corner a sign hung which was the advertisement of a notorious crimp, a sailor's boarding-house keeper, whose establishment was on the *bocca* for years. An old sailor who was working in the scene and who had lived in Buenos Aires came to me and said: 'I've been shanghaied by that bloodsucker'.

I have gone so far as to have my principals speak the language of the country in which the picture is laid. Few of them like to go to this trouble, but it helps them materially in keeping to the required atmosphere. The results on the screen are so encouraging that, after they see what it has done for them, the players don't mind the extra study this course entails.

I know of no branch of a director's job that is more fascinating than

Opposite: *Ingram and von Stroheim.*

getting colour and atmosphere into the settings — thinking out bits of 'business', little flashes of life which, though only on the screen for a few moments, can give an air of reality to an entire sequence of scenes, that would perhaps otherwise be lacking.

In screening Balzac, as I did in making *The Conquering Power,* fine atmosphere and characterisation are of more vital importance than incident, for nine times out of ten it is the characters in a great novel that we remember — rather than the plot.

Ingram had been working very hard since he started with Metro in 1920. They were mostly large-scale productions and called for intense research and planning. He had many friends in Hollywood but avoided the social round, disliking the dress-suit occasion. His attire was odd and he slouched around in any old thing he could find, usually an old khaki shirt and trousers.

He was a close friend of the Laskys and had designed a white Packard special for Jesse, which Cecil de Mille christened *Corona Corona* because of its long wheel base. The design was inspired by Ralph de Palma's racing car. Rex himself drove and in the old days favoured a Stutz, but later switched to Ford. He and Griffith admired each other's work and the latter always referred to Rex as 'one of my boys' although Rex never actually worked with him.

Von Stroheim was another friend and, when it came to reducing *Greed* from its original forty reels to half that length, Rex was the only one von Stroheim would trust with his precious film. The cutting was done by Grant Whytock, who had a formidable task, since the pattern of the film was closely knit and to tamper with one part was to produce detrimental repercussions in another part. One whole story of the relations of Maria Macapa and Zerkow, the junkman, was eliminated and the remainder trimmed to make a two-part film. Whytock was tremendously impressed with von Stroheim's original. Ingram wrote to von Stroheim that if he allowed MGM to cut another inch he would never speak to him again. Alas, the two-part version was scrapped and the film issued in a severely mutilated ten-reel version.

Ingram was keenly interested in the developments of the European cinema. He was familiar with the pioneer work of Victor Sjöström whom he met in Hollywood, and he invited Paul Wegener to work with him after seeing *The Golem.* It was not convenient at the time, but later Wegener did act for Ingram at the Nice studios.

In his old Universal days Rex lived at the famous Hollywood Hotel, through which passed many a famous director. After the war he moved to the Hotel Christy on Hollywood Boulevard and in late 1918 he lived at 2041 Pinehurst Road, where he was looked after by the kindly Elizabeth Waggoner at a most difficult period in his life. He and Alice Terry moved to 1509 Cassell Place, Hollywood, subsequently residing at Whitley Terrace and a house off Vine Street, which belonged at one time to James Cruze.

Rex did not neglect his sculpture. His interest in the art world was stimulated by his correspondence with his old teacher Lee Lawrie. His collection of paintings and *objets d'art* reflected impeccable taste and his contact with Arab culture proved a further incentive.

Up to this time he had many unrealised projects. Towards the end of 1921

Mal St Clair, D. W. Griffith and Rex Ingram.

he was planning a production of *Ivanhoe* to be shot in England, with Alice Terry as Rowena. He was deeply interested in Jacob Wasserman's *Christian Wahnschaffe,* a Dostoievsky-like novel of a wealthy young idealist who tries to reconcile the problems of poverty and suffering. This was a vast canvas of life and character. The book had originally been bought by Metro for Nazimova. Ingram got the rights and under the English title of *The World's Illusion* intended to film it. Willis Goldbeck wrote the script in 1923 and it was thought that Ingram himself might play the lead opposite Jetta Goudal. A two-part film had been made in Germany in 1921-2 by Urban Gad with Lillebil Ibsen, Conrad Veidt, Fritz Kortner, Werner Krauss and Rosel Mueller. It may have been the discovery of this German version which caused Ingram to suspend his plans.

Hugo's *Toilers of the Sea* was to have been filmed in Florida after *Where the Pavement Ends.* Novarro and Antonio Moreno were mentioned for the leads. Kamuela Searle, an athlete, sculptor and octopus-catcher from Hawaii, was also being considered. He had gained film experience as an extra. But the film was eventually made by R. William Neill in Italy and released in the United States in 1923.

A plan to film de Maupassant's *Boule de Suif* with von Stroheim as the Prussian officer came to nothing. Other subjects which interested Rex were Wasserman's *The Goose Man,* Blasco Ibáñez's *The Dead Command* and Marion

Crawford's *A Cigarette Maker's Romance.*

On the eve of his departure for Europe Ingram had prestige and international fame and was the highest-paid director in Hollywood. Writing of him in 1923 Robert Florey said: 'Rex Ingram is one of the best living directors. In America he is mentioned next in place to Griffith. Although less well-known in France, the Parisian public have come to appreciate him through *The Four Horsemen of the Apocalypse, Eugénie Grandet, Trifling Women* and *The Prisoner of Zenda* . . . Rex Ingram is expected to become one of the most famous directors in the world – and soon.' He adds: 'Rex Ingram is a most affable and sympathetic man.'

Ingram's films were nearly always included in the ten best of the year. In 1924 in the *Film Daily* poll for the best director, the top three included James Cruze, Cecil de Mille and Rex Ingram. In the same year *Photoplay* listed Cecil de Mille, Griffith and Rex Ingram as their choice. These polls represented a nationwide choice. Armed with these credentials the Ingrams set out to establish a new Hollywood in Europe.

The Rex Ingram Studios, Nice.

10 The King of Nice

In a western suburb of Nice there is a hill which rises above the little railway station of St Augustine. As you climb the hill there is a splendid view of the Baie des Anges. Today the view is more restricted than in 1924 when Ingram chose this site for his European studios. Here, he hoped, he could work free from the Hollywood business controls and in an atmosphere more congenial to his health and temperament.

The site was once the estate of General Massena, Napoleon's general and later Prince d'Essling. The grounds had become a market garden, but here in 1917 Louis Nalpas built a film studio called the Victorine Studios, after the hill on which it stands. By 1924 this had become derelict and was in the hands of the receivers. In the centre was the former Villa Massena, known today as the Villa Rex.

When Rex first saw them, the tall ateliers looked gaunt and tawdry as they stood backed by the cypresses and tombstones of the nearby cemetery. Glass roofs invited the sun to shine into the ghostly interiors from which the directors and mimes had vanished.

Nice was a picturesque and lively city. It was centrally situated in the Mediterranean and within easy reach of Spain, France, Italy and North Africa. The climate was bright and sunny and yet it was possible to obtain snowy landscapes in the nearby Alps. The variety of its environment and hinterland were very tempting to the film-maker.

Its tradition of film-making began as early as 1912 when Charles Burguet founded the Société des Films Azur and made some fourteen films. Louis Nalpas first operated from the Villa Liserb, until with the co-operation of Serge Sandberg, a wealthy and enlightened industrialist, he built the Victorine Studios. Nice produced many famous films: René le Somptier's *Sultane d'Amour* of which Burguet was co-director and Marco de Gastyne art director; *L'Atre* by Boudrioz; Germaine Dulac's *La Fête Espagnol*; Fescourt's *Mathias Sandorf*; Toussaint's *Tristan et Iseult*; and Gérard Bourgeois's *Christophe Colombe*. Jean Durand made comedies with Marcel Levesque, and Gaby Morlay appeared in the films of Charles Burguet. Feuillade died here on 26 February 1925, while making his last film.

In Paris, during the making of *The Arab,* Ingram met old Hollywood friends like Jean de Limur and new acquaintances like Harry Lachman and Max de Vaucorbeil. Lachman introduced him to the cultural life of France. Lachman recalls: 'I met Rex in Paris at my exhibition of paintings at the Galerie Bernheim; he purchased one of the paintings and invited me to dinner. He said he was going to Nice to make *Mare Nostrum* with Tony Moreno and Alice

Rex and Alice at Nice.

MARE NOSTRUM, *Metro-Goldwyn 1926. Uni Apollon (left) and Abd-el-Kader.*

Terry. He asked me to go with him to help him get located as none of the staff spoke French. After several weeks of inactivity in Nice I told Rex I was returning to my Paris Studio. He insisted that I stay on a while longer. I told him I would first rent a studio in Nice — the Victorine — but it was tied up by the creditors and couldn't be rented. I hired a French lawyer, Edouard Corniglion-Molinier, and we went to Paris and managed to untie the studio. When we returned to Nice Rex asked me if I would like to take over the management of the entire affair.' And so Harry Lachman became production manager for Rex Ingram Productions.

The making of *Mare Nostrum* and the equipment of the Victorine Studios went hand in hand. Not always too comfortably, however: the trial and error inevitable in such an undertaking slowed down production. Ingram was driven by the desire to repeat his success with the previous Blasco Ibáñez subject and to capture the mystery of the Mediterranean with which he had fallen in love. Filming proceeded under grim conditions. The glass roofs of the studio created a furnace in the daytime, while, at night, when a lot of the filming took place, arctic temperatures were recorded. The lighting system left a lot to be desired and it was taking time for the crews of French, Italian and American technicians to get to know each other. The laboratory problem was another item to be reckoned with. French laboratories for printing film were found to

ER · AMPHITRI

MARE NOSTRUM, *Metro-Goldwyn, 1926. Painting by Pablo Arranican of Alice Terry as the Goddess Amphitrite* (opposite); *the symbolic love scene in the aquarium* (top); *John George, Rosita Garcia, Hughie Mack and Shorty Ben Mairech* (bottom).

be unsatisfactory. The London laboratories were too far away. Equipment set up in the studios developed defects and much negative was found to be unusable and necessitated many retakes of scenes. Eventually technicians had to be brought from Hollywood for this work. Production expenses were high because they included the cost of modernising the studios. Many of the shots, however, were economical model shots.

Ben Carré, the eminent art director, worked on the film until he clashed with Ingram and was removed. Ingram himself then took on the role of art director, giving sketches of the scenes to Seitz, who had to parley with French and Italian construction men. Language difficulties on all sides slowed production.

While Nice was well equipped with antique shops and sources of material required for film production, unfortunately the relations between tradespeople

MARE NOSTRUM, *Metro-Goldwyn, 1926. The* Mare Nostrum.

and film companies had not been very good in the past, and much haggling was necessary to meet the requirements of *Mare Nostrum*. Extras were no problem. Many of Nice's large Russian emigré population, including dukes and princes, were glad to get any means of livelihood.

Meanwhile, the production of *Ben Hur* was coming to an ignominious end in Rome. Ingram visited Italy, returning with a haul of generators and lighting equipment as well as many technicians. Amleto Negri, one of them, is working at the Victorine to this day.

Ingram's good relations with both French army and government enabled him to obtain men and two submarines for the sea scenes which formed so important a part of the film. One of the submarines was the *Paul Rodier*; both had been captured from the Germans in World War I. Ingram, like von Stroheim, was fascinated by uniforms and had a passion for authenticity. A Spanish fishing vessel was acquired for the important role of Captain Ferragut's *Mare Nostrum*.

The difficulties of some of the scenes may be indicated by those encountered in filming the sinking of the submarine. Hordes of white Russians were used for this. They had to plunge into icy waters, fortified on each occasion by a nip of vodka. They kept going back into the sea again and again until they ended up petrified by the cold.

Submarine scenes were filmed at Toulon and Villefranche. On one occasion off Toulon the camera crew were almost a target for nearby naval manoeuvres. Ingram favoured afternoon shooting to get the best light effects. The greatest care was taken to get exactly what he wanted and he repeated and repeated scenes until everything was right. One scene called for the use of octopi: hundreds of the creatures were sacrificed to the perfection of the shot. In another scene, the symbolic hand of death wipes out the name of the ship written across the wall of life. Ingram shot this 185 times. Time and effort were certainly not spared. A tank was built in the studios for the underwater scenes and much ingenuity was required to obtain the effects called for. Among the experts Ingram engaged was Walter Pallman who did the trick miniatures and ceilings, including the little horses for the allegorical scenes of Amphitrite and Neptune. The portrait of Alice Terry as Amphitrite included in the film was painted by the Spanish artist Pablo Arranican.

Apart from the complicated sea scenes and even underwater scenes, the production was on so large a scale that it required locations in three countries — France, Spain and Italy. The Spanish scenes shot in Barcelona by John Seitz included those outside the cathedral with Moreno. Ingram did not go to Spain and according to John Seitz he revealed a jealousy which strained the good relations between the two men. Ingram did, however, travel to Naples, Pompeii and Paestum for the Italian scenes. Extensive use was made of the southern French coast.

The story of *Mare Nostrum* was based on Vicente Blasco Ibáñez's novel of love and espionage in the Mediterranean during World War I. Ulysses Ferragut, the Spanish captain of a sailing ship, the *Mare Nostrum*, falls in love with Freya Talberg, a beautiful woman working for the Germans. He is induced to help refuel German submarines in the Mediterranean. When his son is lost on a ship torpedoed by one of these submarines he swears vengeance and loses his life

MARE NOSTRUM, *Metro-Goldwyn 1926. Alice Terry as Freya.*

destroying the enemy. Freya is betrayed by her own organisation to the French and is shot as a spy. The subsidiary mystical theme has Freya, symbolising the goddess Amphitrite, reunited with Ulysses in death.

A great deal of the value of the film depended on the casting and here Ingram selected his people very carefully. First, of course, came Alice Terry who was to give the performance of her career as Freya. She had previously played *ingenue* roles and here was a mature intellectual woman of great personality and beauty. Alice rose to the challenge. 'I feel that *Mare Nostrum* was the only film I ever did really.' It was not an easy role and there were technical problems. About the scene in which Freya and Ulysses make love in front of the glass tank containing an octopus in the Naples Aquarium, Alice told Rex, 'You'd better get rid of me now because I'm not going to be able to do that aquarium scene. I can't look amorous with a big fish doing this by the side of my head.' But Rex deferred the shooting of the scene. On the day they did shoot it Alice's heart was in her mouth expecting retake after retake. To Alice's great amazement, Rex said: 'That's it' on the first shot. She summed up her thoughts about it when she said, 'I will never get another part like that, I will never like a part better and I will never have the luck I had on that.'

Ferragut was played by Antonio Moreno, a Spanish actor who had a most successful career in films and later directed the first Mexican sound-film. The other players formed a strange assemblage. Uni Apollon, the Triton, had a strong-man act at the Folies Bergères. Mlle Kithnou as Ulysses' wife was a dancer from the island of Mauritius. The great fat Irish Hughie Mack played Caragol, the ship's cook. Mme Paquerette played the lesbian Dr Fedelmann, but the most striking acquisition was the sinister bald-headed Andrews Engelmann for the role of the German submarine commander.

Engelmann relates that he 'first met Rex Ingram in Paris in 1924 at Louis P. Verande, my manager's office. Rex was then casting *Mare Nostrum*. He entered the room, had a short look at me and then said OK to Verande and off he went . . . What struck me most when arriving in Nice was Rex Ingram's car. Rex was riding on a chassis of a Rolls, or something of that kind, with just two basket chairs tied to this chassis with leather straps, without any kind of body . . . during my different stays in Nice, I never saw Rex Ingram dressed otherwise than in military shirts and pants.

The casualness of his dress puzzled many of his friends. Lachman said: 'One of Rex's peculiarities was his liking to dress like a bum. Old sloppy clothes, no socks and open sandals. On the trip we took to New York on a luxury liner with the great lawyer, Nathan Burkan (Rex's lawyer), Rex appeared for supper in the sloppy clothes and no socks. I heard a couple of husky Americans say, "We ought to beat that fellow up." I told Rex, and the next day he appeared in a tuxedo, impeccable and of course handsome.'

The script for *Mare Nostrum* was written by Willis Goldbeck. John Seitz, who had been loaned by Ingram to Jules Brulatour for his 1924 *Price of a Party*, came from Hollywood to work on the film. Joe Boyle came along, but not Curt Rehfeld, who had now become a director on his own and made *The Greater Glory* for First National with Anna Q. Nilsson in the lead and with a script by June Mathis.

Credits on Ingram films are skimpy and vague. The words production

MARE NOSTRUM, *Metro-Goldwyn 1926*. Above:*Freya goes to her execution.*
Opposite:*the author Blasco Ibáñez reads the script; with him are Antonio Moreno, Ingram and Alice Terry.*

technical or executive can cover anything. We know for instance that Jean de Limur, Max de Vaucorbeil and many others worked on *Mare Nostrum* without a credit.

John George played in the film, but annoyed Ingram by extensive gambling and was given his fare back to the States. Abd-el-Kadar, the boy adopted by the Ingrams, played Ulysses Ferragut as a child. For the role of Ulysses' son, Ingram wanted the brilliant French boy actor, Jean Forest, but his contract with Jacques Feyder did not allow him to accept the offer. The part went to the English Mickey Brantford.

Alice Terry did not appear in Nice until well on in the production as, towards the end of 1924, she was making *Confessions of a Queen* for Victor Sjöström, *The Great Divide* for Reginald Barker and *Sackcloth and Ashes* and *Any Woman* for Henry King. When she arrived in Nice the Ingram residence was at the Hotel Ruhl, although Rex lived almost entirely in the villa attached to the studio.

Blasco Ibáñez took a personal interest in the production. Alice Terry liked him: 'Blasco Ibáñez used to come to the studio all the time and he was very nice and I liked him because he didn't say I was the wrong type, and he didn't look on me as though I was going to ruin the story. He was very pleasant and his wife came along and we used to go over to their place at Menton (the Villa

Rosa) and have lunch and it was all very agreeable.'

By May of 1925 the sea scenes had been organised at Toulon and Ville-franche. At the latter town Alice Terry was made an honorary Colonel of the 24th Battalion de Chasseurs Alpins, better known as 'The Blue Devils', who themselves appeared in the film.

Jean de Limur said: 'Rex was quite stubborn. When he had an idea to shoot a scene in a certain place, there was nothing that could be done about it. He just had to do it and he did it. Nobody could cross him. He was his own producer. Of course it cost an awful lot of money. We stayed at Nice and there was a scene to be shot at Frejus which was fifty-five kilometres from Nice across the mountains, and we travelled by road. Every morning the company would leave Nice for Frejus at 8 a.m. on a two-hours trip. We would shoot then whether it was good or not. Sometimes we would not shoot at all. We would have to wait all day for the sunshine and then come back to Nice.'

Andrews Engelmann has this to say: 'Rex knew what he wanted and visualised it. Most of the film directors of those days made their films without a real script, but Rex Ingram knew what he was going to shoot. Scripts were handed to the actors, scenes were discussed and psychologically and figuratively conceived in connection with the dramatic structure of the whole film.'

The film took fifteen months to make and the editing was a huge under-taking. Drastic elimination of material was necessary. Like *Greed,* whole

Above: *Ingram checks with his editor, Grant Whytock.*
Opposite: *The première of* MARE NOSTRUM *at the Criterion Theatre, New York.*

sequences and subsidiary stories were removed. Grant Whytock estimated that
the first cut came to 23,000 ft. 'We must have thrown away ten or twelve cut
reels and we still landed up with two and a half hours of film.' The negative was
cut in France and some sample prints were made from a beautiful Belgian stock
with a kind of sepia toning. Whytock also estimates that over a million feet
were shot for the film. 'Rex never really made anything that would not cut
because he shot an enormous amount of coverage . . . We used to print two and
three takes of things. Today we don't do that.' Ingram used the Urbagraph
laboratories in New York for the final prints. The rejection of so much of his
material for the film must have been distressing to Rex who asked Whytock to
let him know in advance of proposed cuts. Whytock sympathised with him and
softened the blow as best he could. Like two other masterpieces which were
drastically abbreviated for commercial release — *Greed* and *The Gösta Berling
Saga* — *Mare Nostrum* may have lost a dimension. Cutting was not always a
serious business, however, for Whytock once cut in scenes of the Roman galleys
from the *Ben Hur* production into the submarine sequence from *Mare Nostrum*
with devastatingly funny results. The footage shot in Rome for *Ben Hur*
found its way to the Rex Ingram Studios and Whytock insists that not a foot

Ingram and Matisse.

of the Italian material from that film was ever used in the final version which was entirely shot in Hollywood.

A much abbreviated version of *Mare Nostrum* had its première at the Criterion Theatre, New York on 15 February 1926. On the whole it had an excellent reception in what was, for MGM, a vintage year, with Niblo's *Ben Hur,* Vidor's *Big Parade* and *La Bohème* running almost simultaneously.

Blasco Ibáñez saw it much earlier, for in his letter of 21 October 1925 he writes: 'I personally thank you for the wonderful way in which you have interpreted my novel. Of all the stories I have written, *Mare Nostrum* is my favourite. For that reason, only to a great artist like yourself could I trust it to be put into motion pictures.' Having praised the film in all its aspects, he gave special mention to the authenticity of Alice Terry's interpretation of Freya Talberg.

The critics wrote extensively about it. Richard Watts Jr in the *Herald Tribune* spoke of its fine directorial skill. C. S. Sewell in the *Moving Picture World* said: 'Mr Ingram has undoubtedly produced a big picture. Technically, artistically, from the standpoint of acting, scenic investiture and in the power of its theme and the sincerity with which it has been transferred to the screen without compromising with the conventional it is superb . . . It is the kind of film that will be widely discussed.' Cedric Belfrage in *Picturegoer*: 'It is a very remarkable production with which there can be no doubt that Ingram makes an artistic come-back, if not a commercial one . . . It leaves the spectator with

The Villa Rex.

much the same mixed feelings as Stroheim's *Greed*. The photography of *Mare Nostrum* is exquisite and the acting brilliant, Antonio Moreno, especially revealing an undreamt-of dramatic ability.' And in Ingram's native Dublin the *Evening Herald* wrote: '*Mare Nostrum* is easily the finest picture that has been released this year to the Dublin picture-goers. Rex Ingram has again found inspiring material for a big production in the Blasco Ibáñez story. He seems to be one of the few producers who can preserve the spirit of the author's story while producing from it something entirely original for the screen.'

In Paris the film opened before a glittering audience which included the French Premier. Shortly after, on 15 August 1926, Ingram was made a Chevalier of the Legion of Honour. The previous day the same order was con-ferred on another great man of the cinema, Marcel l'Herbier. They were probably the first film people to be so honoured and Ingram must certainly have been the youngest to receive it.

But not all was plain sailing. James R. Quirke of *Photoplay* disliked the film and waxed moralistic. 'Not only is the picture a great dramatic disappoint-ment, but there are episodes in it of a suggestive perversity that will detract from the reputation of this director.' This was typical of the reactions of the Hollywood chauvinists of the Louella Parsons school. However, *Photoplay* selected Alice Terry's performance as one of the six best of the year.

Blasco Ibáñez was very anti-German in his writings and this aspect is endorsed by Ingram in the films. Neither *The Four Horsemen of the Apocalypse* nor *Mare Nostrum* were shown in Germany. In September 1926 the first International Film Congress, sponsored by the League of Nations, condemned inflammatory films, and as *The Four Horsemen* had many revivals, particularly after the death of Valentino, it had achieved a certain notoriety in relation to these protests. Ludwig Scheer, the President of the National Association of German Cinema-owners, called for a ban on the film in all European countries in an article in *Film Kurier* on 4 October 1926. On 11 November (Armistice Day) of the same year the German ambassador in Washington protested at the continued showing of the film. Pressures were also applied in England. Letters in the press and parliamentary discussion focussed attention on films which perpetuated national hatreds.

The official endorsement of *Mare Nostrum* by French government circles and the association with it of Georges Leygues, Minister for the Navy, infuriated Germany and further protests were lodged. The film was heavily cut for distribution purposes in France and this lessened its chances of commercial success. MGM was running a risk of German boycott of its films. After a time *Mare Nostrum* was withdrawn as well as *The Four Horsemen*. In England even the film on Edith Cavell, *Dawn*, featuring Sybil Thorndike was banned. The controversy continued for a few years for according to the London *Times* of 24 February 1928: 'The American film *Mare Nostrum* dealing with sub-marine warfare which had a long and successful circulation was withdrawn at the beginning of the year because it was then thought that it might give offence on the Continent. There was no official interference in the matter of any kind. The same applies to the cession of re-issues of *The Four Horsemen of the Apocalypse,* first produced more than five years ago.'

Opening shots of waves washing against a rocky coast are followed by these

Ingram the boxer.

titles: 'Between Europe and Africa stretching from Gibraltar to the Syrian Coast, lies the Mediterranean, land-locked and tideless, known to the ancients as *Mare Nostrum — Our Sea* . . . Upon its bosom mankind spread the first sail, from its depths the seagods were born.' Ingram weaves his evocative magic to the very end when the lovers are re-united in death: 'Conscious no longer, seeing her with eyes now closed forever . . . in his heart a voice crying to her: Freya . . . Amphitrite.' And the waves again beat against the rocks. I think it was my friend Herman Weinberg who described it as a love-poem to the Mediterranean, a sad tragic story of an inflexible destiny told in images of great beauty. When the spy is chased through the streets of the French town or the ship sails across the blue water or the spirit of the ancient gods breathes over the ruins of Paestum and Pompeii one is impressed with the rich texture which Ingram has wrought. The execution of Freya at the hands of the French firing squad at dawn is one of the most moving sequences Ingram ever achieved. The types and characters depicted in the film are part of the mood and feeling. Herman Weinberg chose two unforgettable images from it: 'The goddess Amphitrite riding the waves of the sea on a dolphin during a luminous night, watched by Neptune on a rock on the shore — and the epilogue of the drowned lovers meeting and forever in the depths of the sea.' He goes on, '*Mare Nostrum* also contains a rendezvous in an aquarium before a tank containing an octopus

THE MAGICIAN, *Metro-Goldwyn 1926. Alice Terry and Stowitts.*

THE MAGICIAN, *Metro-Goldwyn 1926. Paul Wegener in the title role.*

A studio illusion. Seated in foreground John Seitz and Firmin Gemier. Behind them Harry Lachm

(overtonal montage within the frame) which was the progenitor of Orson Welles's rendezvous of the lovers in *Lady from Shanghai,* also in an aquarium, this time before a tank containing a huge predatory fish.'

Ingram fought to retain the original Blasco Ibáñez title in its Latin form. He also held out for the tragic ending as he had always resisted the cliché ending, regarded by some producers as a formula for box-office success. The death of Julio in *The Four Horsemen,* the broken romance of Rassendyll in *Zenda,* the final holocaust of *Trifling Women* and the death leap in the waterfall from *Where the Pavement Ends* did not pander to audience preferences.

The studio was originally taken over by MGM with an option to purchase and during the production of *Mare Nostrum* it was modernised as well as equipped. Nicholas Schenck, however, did not wish to acquire foreign property for his company and the option was transferred to Ingram, on the understanding that two-thirds of the improvements be paid back to MGM. There was some difficulty about the 25 per cent foreign purchase tax, but eventually Ingram became owner of the studios for $5 million and rented them to MGM for their subsequent productions. The thought of Ingram hiring out to Louis B. Mayer studios which Mayer had already paid for made von Stroheim smile. All of Ingram's affairs were handled by Corniglion Molinier on a very loose and ultimately disastrous basis for Ingram.

John Seitz disapproved of Rex involving himself with the burden of the studio, but remained to work with him on his next picture, Somerset Maugham's *The Magician,* based on a tale of a sinister occultist with an almost Svengali-like domination over the mind of the heroine. It became a struggle between good and evil and had a mad scientist, a Dracula-like castle and erotic dream sequences, very much a precursor of the horror films so popular in the cinema in recent times. The central character was based on the notorious Aleistar Crowley. This role was played by the German actor Paul Wegener and indeed the film took on something of the macabre atmosphere of so many German films of the twenties. It was not a good film, having a weak story line with some bad sagging in the middle. But it had moments of the old Ingram magic. The dénouement in the Magician's lair, the operation scenes and the satyric orgies were memorable and one regrets the waste of many scenes which were beautiful to look at.

It is perhaps Alice Terry's least effective part. Her make-up left a lot to be desired and the heroine emerges as rather colourless. Firmin Gemier of the Comedie Francaise, who had a not entirely successful tour of the States, played the sympathetic Dr Porhoet and was given $12,000 by Ingram, who also used him in the capacity of assistant. He had played as early as 1912 in Andreani's *L'Homme Qui Assassina,* but had not appeared again in films until Gance's *Master Dolorosa* in 1917. Ivan Petrovitch, a young Serb from Novy Sad, was a new Ingram acquisition who eventually played in three films for him. He had already appeared in Austrian, German and French films including Germaine Dulac's *Ame d'Artiste,* de Gastyne's *Chatelaine du Liban* and Perret's *Koenigsmark.* The part of the faun, which was originally to have been played by Serge Lifar, was taken by Stowitts, a former partner of Anna Pavlova.

Henri Menessier, the designer, who came to Ingram at the end of *Mare Nostrum* had worked with Nazimova in Hollywood, notably on Capellani's *The Red Lantern* (1919). The great statue of Pan was created by Paul Dardé and executed in the studio workshops by the Italian plaster workers whom Ingram had engaged. The sorcerer's tower was built in the village of Sospel in the mountains behind Nice and locations used included the Dome, the Café Royale and the Parc Monceau in Paris, and Monte Carlo, Nice and Cannes.

It opened at the Criterion Theatre, New York on 24 October 1926. The *Moving Picture World* described it as 'exciting, if gruesome, entertainment excellently handled'. But apart from appreciation of its attractive pictorial quality it cannot claim to have been successful.

The shooting of the fantasy scenes of the naked faun and the nymphs were staged in the neighbourhood of Nice and did nothing to improve the opinions of the staid citizens about the carryings-on of those wicked film people.

Ingram himself had adapted Maugham's story to the screen and this led to enmity between the author and his interpreter, Ingram claiming that he did his best with a not very good story.

Wegener was not very popular with his colleagues. Seitz regarded him as a ham, and the others resented his pomposity. He had his own make-up man, whom he screamed at on the slightest provocation.

About this time Ingram toyed with a project which must have seemed very attractive to him. The origin of the word 'lynching' is supposed to come from the story of a Mayor Lynch of Galway City, who, some centuries ago was said to have hanged his son from the window of his house. The young man had killed a Spanish youth in a jealous rage, but he was so popular with everyone that nobody would carry out the sentence. His stern old father took the law into his own hands, thereby giving a new word to the English language. Ingram planned to have Blasco Ibáñez write the script, but it remained just a project.

Ingram had arrived in Nice with a grandiose scheme to establish a European Hollywood and with a legendary reputation as the director of much publicised films, as the discoverer of Valentino and Novarro and as a colourful and attractive personality. With the foundation and ownership of the Rex Ingram Studios, Nice regarded him as one of its greatest assets. He added to the city's film-making reputation, he provided employment and he was world news: His visitors sound like a *Who's Who* of the twenties. Writers like Bernard Shaw, the Scott Fitzgeralds, John Galsworthy, Blasco Ibáñez, Pierre Benoit, Michael Arlen, James Barrie, Robert Hichens, Cosmo Hamilton were received by him. Even Frank Harris. Film colleagues who dropped in were Chaplin, James Cruze, Adolphe Menjou, King Vidor, Valentino, Pearl White, Leslie Henson, Syd Chaplin, Douglas Fairbanks and Mary Pickford. Fairbanks said the Ingram Studios were the best in Europe after the famous UFA in Berlin. Politicians and royalty, too, came to pay court to the King of Nice. When the Duke of Connaught visited him Rex went to some trouble to fly an Irish tricolour over the studio.

During the period of *The Magician* the Ingrams stayed in the Hotel Negresco. Isadora Duncan was then enjoying there the hospitality of the management, who did not dare throw out such a distinguished artist for non-payment of bills. They later moved to the Palais Los Angeles, and the Villa Binh Hoa and spent some time in 3 rue Cronstadt. While Alice lived her own life more or less independently, Rex centred his activities in the villa at the studios. Here he was served by the old fisherman Thibaut, who was his cook and general factotum. The villa was decorated with the Moorish *objets d'art* which he had collected and with paintings by Dinet, a French painter who had abandoned Western ways to live as a brother amongst the Arabs. North Africa fascinated Ingram and he studied Arabic, and was visited by Arab friends including El Glaoui and the Bey of Tunis. A personal jester, Shorty Ben Mairech given to him by the Bey, appeared in many of Rex's films and was often the butt of his bad temper.

Rex liked shooting in the afternoon to get certain light-values into his films. This left the morning free for swimming and sunbathing at the Grande Bleue. He was an excellent swimmer and once saved a man and a boy from drowning. He was flattered by the attention he aroused in young women. He was of an amiable disposition and very fond of children. But he could also retire into himself and become a recluse. He had a boyish arrogance and could be aggressive if he so wished. He kept up his boxing and had regular sparring partners, including a Spanish champion named Tommy Cola. Once, when a man insulted Alice and the wife of his friend George Busby on the beach, he had a fight arranged between the man and George.

M. Pouchet, one of the studio's business administrators, lost patience with Rex's nature cult when Rex was missing for an important business conference.

He might be having breakfast with his friends or stretching himself in the sun on the beach. In the meantime things could be hung up at the studio.

Sewell Stokes in his book *Pilloried* mentions meeting Ingram at a dance hall where he was foxtrotting. 'He had a kind of boyish face, wore a khaki shirt open at the neck and a noticeably gold bracelet to his wrist watch . . . Mr Ingram did not strike me as being the least conceited. Quite the reverse. Suddenly, as if tiring of the dancing crowd, which had not left its beach tactics behind it, he made a hasty departure. Through the open night of the dance hall I watched him walk into the night. For a few seconds he looked up to where the moon with tipsy eyes looked back at him out of a deep blue sky. Then he crossed the road, climbed into his little car and drove towards the hills, where, hidden behind palms and cypresses, stood the studio that was also his home.'

Stokes visited him in his villa and found him most affable. 'He looked so bored, poor man, that I was genuinely sorry for him. Gone now were those feelings of resentment which had assailed me when it seemed impossible to get near the man. Now that I was alone with him I could afford to feel sorry, could understand his great need of protection from the mob.' He spoke about amending Maugham's *The Magician* and about film endings in general. He disagreed with C. W. Nevinson's remark that *Zenda* was better than anything Griffith had done. He led Sewell through the villa whose rooms were restfully simple in character. He proudly called attention to Sodoma's painting of an Arab boy and to a less skilled but authentic picture of San Francisco's China-town. His sculptures stood around the room. When shown an unfavourable American criticism of *Mare Nostrum* he just shrugged his shoulders: 'I think the Americans are sick with me for producing films out of Hollywood. They like money to come into their own country, not to leave it.' He confessed to reading very little and was only interested in the stories he read in his youth. Sewell noted that only one of the stories he filmed was in existence when he was a boy.

Just before he tackled his next film, Robert Hichen's *The Garden of Allah*, many changes in the pattern of Ingram's life came about. John Seitz, his cameraman, with whom relations were none too good, decided to return to Hollywood as did Grant Whytock, his editor. Seitz said 'I had become tired of working in France and felt if I stayed much longer I would have little or no career left when I returned to Hollywood, so, much as I regretted to leave Ingram after our years together, I felt that I must. He made *The Garden of Allah* after I left. This was his last picture for Metro. I thought it a very good picture. After this he did two pictures, one of which I saw and regret to say it was not good, especially being a silent picture, when they were no longer made here. The other picture which I did not see had sound, but Rex told me later that he had so much trouble with the sound equipment that he was discouraged — he actually did not like sound pictures anyway. This to me was a tragedy. Here was a young man of thirty-six, who had so many successes, giving up motion pictures at a time when most directors were just getting a start.'

But we anticipate. The next film scheduled was *The Garden of Allah* for which he engaged Lee Garmes, a cameraman noted for his rich pictorial quality and atmospheric photography. Garmes had started his career in films in 1916 and had worked with Thomas H. Ince and latterly with Mal St Clair. He later

THE GARDEN OF ALLAH, *Metro-Goldwyn 1927. The monastery of Staoueli.*

worked with von Sternberg and brought some of what he learned from Ingram to the films of Marlene Dietrich. Ingram, with his cameraman Seitz, set high standards in the field of cinematography. Seitz favoured the use of Rembrandt's north light and experimented with panchromatic film.

In an interview with Charles Higham, Garmes speaks of his assignment: 'Ingram was a perfectionist, who kept hounding me and hounding me to follow the style of John Seitz who had been with him before; Johnny didn't use any rim lights or back lights, anything like that. He had a north-light effect on his faces, and Rex wanted that; I gave it to him, and I fell in love with north-light, and used it as my signature. Only Johnny, Vic Milner and I were using north-light; we put it on the map. Like Mal, Rex was a painter and understood what I was doing. I started off by doing *The Garden of Allah* for him; Alice Terry was fine, and I loved working with them.'

The Garden of Allah marked the turning point in Ingram's career. On its completion his contract with MGM was not renewed. A great deal of strife smouldered underneath the production. It led to departures, much bitterness and alienation of friends. Finally the beloved studio, the Victorine, passed out of his control. Even then Ingram kept things moving, not failing to astonish with his personal idiosyncrasies and grand manner.

While the film was in preparation, Alice Terry returned to Hollywood to play with Ramon Novarro in *Lovers,* based on Echegaray's *The Great Galeotto.* This was directed by John Stahl. Valentino had died on 15 August 1926 and June Mathis, who had played such an important part in Ingram's career and who was perhaps the most intelligent scriptwriter in Hollywood, died suddenly while she was attending a theatre in New York on 26 July 1927. During her distinguished lifetime she wrote *An Eye for an Eye* and *The Red Lantern* for Nazimova, both directed by Capellani, the two Valentino films for Ingram and the other Valentino films *Blood and Sand* and *The Young Rajah,* the final version of *Greed* by von Stroheim, *Ben Hur* for Fred Niblo, *The Greater Glory* for Curt Rehfeld and *The Magic Flame* for Henry King. She was buried in her own vault in Hollywood Cemetery beside Valentino.

In New York City, Marcus Loew, Ingram's patron, had died on 6 September 1926. Loew once said 'I still love that crazy Irishman even if he did cost me ten million dollars by driving Valentino out of our studio.' In fact it was Ingram who had brought Valentino into the studio, and his departure was not entirely due to their quarrel.

Ingram's aggressive side was to develop with the disappointment over losing the direction of *Ben Hur.* Seitz said, 'He received a sudden change in personality. Everything had been going so well for him that this came as a real shock.' De Limur said of him 'He had a bad temper. He didn't like people very much. He was like a recluse. He was a sort of outsider. He wouldn't mingle with the others. He was not friendly at all with anybody. And he was peculiar.' This does not tally with other opinions.

Frank Scully in his book *Cross My Heart* again denigrates Ingram. Scully had been his publicity man on *The Garden of Allah.* He was a devout Catholic and, I suspect, a rather narrow-minded one. He seriously advances the theory that Ingram wanted to make *Allah* because the monk in it has a bastard child. He was wounded by Ingram's boasts of his abandonment of Christianity. He

510

mentions also that things were not going too well with the film and neither Ingram, Alice Terry or MGM were happy with the first rough cut.

Rex's father visited him during the making of the film, and advised on its religious aspects. He was undoubtedly pained by his son's rejection of his Christian upbringing. But there was real affection between father and son. One of the sculptures Rex did at this time was that of a sleeping Christ in the arms of Buddha.

In an article which Rex wrote for the London *Daily Express* of 28 June 1927 he expanded on his personal beliefs, dealing with the sublimity of ignorance and the limits of Man's life-span.

My code of living is to enjoy life while I am here; if possible without causing suffering to others. Life is too short to make others unhappy unless it brings a great deal of happiness to us. In the latter case it depends on our temperament whether or not happiness can be gained in this way.

In order to be happy the mind should be occupied with work or pleasure — I don't think it matters which. Some are fortunate enough to find them identical.

I have never consciously formed a philosophy of life, but I think a sensible one would be the pursuit of happiness. Something very elusive, I realise, but it can be attained if one follows the advice contained in the words, 'Don't Worry'.

Money is only useful up to the point where it can purchase a reasonable amount of independence. After that it becomes more a liability than an asset.

The more money a man accumulates, the more possessions he has, the more of a slave he becomes.

The desert nomad can pack all his earthly goods in a couple of camel bags. He is richer, more free and happier than the richest man in the world.

In the desert all men are free and equal. Their code is the unwritten law of hospitality. Nothing can threaten this freedom, not even Bolshevism, because in threatening there is nothing material to gain; so the personal liberty of the nomad will continue indefinitely.

He goes on to speak of health and the advantage of natural habits and the strain of modern living. He deplores the lack of reflection and the prevalence of bluff and the rat race.

Today respect for mature judgement and age no longer exists as it did. Old age is regarded by modern man as dotage. Today is the time of the young man. But the young man at forty-five is older than his grandfather was at sixty-five . . .

If a man makes up his mind to do one thing to the exclusion of everything else he nearly always accomplishes his purpose, but he must not let the opinion of others, their criticism, friendly or otherwise, unduly influence him.

For my part give me the sun, the sea, enough personal liberty to call my

Opposite: THE GARDEN OF ALLAH, *Metro-Goldwyn 1927. Ivan Petrovitch, Alice Terry and Shorty Ben Mairech.*

time my own, and time enough to do one thing at a time, and satisfy myself that it is being done to the best of my ability.

My ambition in life is to be able to say: 'I have lived well — I have taken all there was to get out of life.'

This didactic piece recalls his father's style, even if the emphasis is somewhat different. It is, we should remember, the utterance of a very wealthy man, and a very successful one. Scully mentions that Rex got $100,000 for the direction of *The Garden of Allah*. Rex himself says he got $125,000 and 25 per cent of the box-office takings. Alice Terry is referred to by Scully as the $30,000 star. Alice in the middle of this crazy world of the Victorine kept her head and advised her more erratic husband to invest his money wisely.

The popular Robert Hichens novel *The Garden of Allah* had previously been filmed in 1916 by Colin Campbell with Helen Ware and Tom Santschi in the leads. It was later filmed by Richard Boleslavsky as a sound film with Marlene Dietrich and Charles Boyer in 1936. The author, however, in his autobiography mentioned that he preferred the Ingram version. It is a tale of a Trappist monk in North Africa, who betrays his vows and flees from his monastery to the desert, where he falls in love with a young Englishwoman. He marries her, but is haunted by a sense of guilt. Trapped in a sandstorm with his wife, he vows that if they are spared he will tell her of his past and return to the monastery. She accepts the situation and will live to devote her life to their son. Her husband resumes his life as a monk.

Alice Terry and Petrovitch were cast as leads. Other players included Claude and Gerald Fielding, Henry Vibart and a young man who had previously appeared in *The Magician* in a small comedy role and who was a sort of general helper around the studios at this time. He was the Michael Powell who later directed such famous films as *I Know Where I'm Going, The Life and Death of Colonel Blimp* and *The Red Shoes*.

Expeditions visited Africa for locations and with Ingram went Harry Lachman, Menessier the designer, Robert Hichens the author, Gerry Fairbanks the make-up man and Rene Bourdin, the medical advisor. Most of the scenes were shot in Biskra in the garden of Count Landon de Longueville, which was some fourteen hours by train from Algiers. It was this garden that had inspired the original story as did Toggourt and the La Trappe Monastery at Staoueli, also used for the film. While shooting, Ingram was once lost in the desert for thirty-six hours.

Lachman refers to Ingram's perfectionism: 'We had a set in a deserted tower in the desert. The prop man shot spider webs around the interior. Rex looked at the set and asked me if I had checked to find if there could be spiders in the desert. I checked this and there could not. So out came the webs. For casting the roles Rex made sketches of the types he wanted and it was up to me to find a near replica. I travelled from Nice to Berlin just to find the type he depicted for a small role. He made drawings of the sets with details of the furnishings. We had to find just such pieces, sometimes going to Paris to rent them.'

There was also the case of a dancer, Rehba, in Tunis who could only be extracted from her husband by payment of a large sum to compensate him for the divorce which was arranged by Rex.

After some re-editing the film opened at the Embassy Theatre, New York, on 2 September 1927. On the whole it achieved a good press and commercial success. The beauty of the desert and its North African exteriors were charmingly revealed in the photography of Lee Garmes. The monastery scenes and the casbahs of the Arab towns contrasted vividly with the sandy dunes and the desert storms. Alice Terry looked serene and beautiful as the heroine, Dominie Enfilden, and the film was filled with studies of strange and unusual people. The *Moving Picture World* called it 'a picture that for sheer beauty of scene has never been equalled'. But it felt that atmosphere and pictorial qualities were achieved at the expense of character. As usual the comedy effects, mainly those with Michael Powell and Paquerette, were strained and naive.

This film completed Ingram's contract with MGM. When he refused to return to Hollywood his contract was not renewed. Louella Parsons wrote in *The American* of 23 July 1927: 'No one can deny that the officials of MGM have had the patience of Job with Rex Ingram. Mr Ingram refused point blank to make his pictures in America, although Marcus Loew pleaded with him to come to Culver City where he would have every facility and co-operation. As I remember the situation, Mr Ingram did a lot of talking about bourgeois America and Hollywood conditions . . . My only surprise is that MGM did not take this stand a long time ago. The pictures turned out in Culver City certainly have never suffered from comparison with Mr Ingram's foreign-made films — and this is no boost for California either.'

Ingram was now his own master. He had bought the studios at the Victorine for $5 million. A prospectus for the studios in 1927 listed the following items:

> Four covered studios with 60,000 square metres of grounds for exteriors.
> Three electric generators giving 3000 amps and three generators giving 9000 amps
> A restaurant to seat 400
> A studio tank with a capacity of 1,300,000 litres
> A modern laboratory
> A studio for model work
> Work shops
> Projection room
> Photographic service
> Editing rooms

MGM officials had from time to time visited the studios and amongst them were Howard Dietz and Howard Strickling, head of MGM publicity, who had known Ingram from the days of *The Four Horsemen*. In later years in a letter to the author Strickling wrote of him: 'He was a pioneer and many years ahead in his thinking and in the making of motion pictures. His *Four Horsemen*, *Scaramouche* and *Mare Nostrum* are still considered masterpieces in the industry. As a man I had great admiration for Mr Ingram. He had integrity and class. He wanted everything the best. He was very opinionated and was the

Above: *The Duke of Connaught at the Ingram Studios.*
Opposite: *The Victorine Studios, Nice, as they are today.*

producer and director of all his pictures and his word was law. The fact that he was not a "yes man" no doubt caused some people not to admire him as much as they might have, although all respected him as a man and as a fine artist."

Now came van Stratton to wind up MGM's affairs in Nice. Back in Hollywood the *Film Daily* included Ingram amongst the ten best directors of 1927 and accorded *The Garden of Allah* a place on its honours list.

On 19 December 1927 G. A. Atkinson, film critic of the *Daily Express,* referred to a letter from Ingram which defended his European Film Scheme and contradicted many rumours prevailing at the time: that he was giving up films to devote himself to sculpture, that he was returning to Hollywood, that he had become a Mohammedan etc. 'For many years I have been interested in things Arabic and have always had a profound respect for Islam,' he said 'I admire much in Islam as I do in Christianity and Buddhism but my sympathy for Islam is rather a question of philosophy of life than faith.'

He answered MGM's charge that films he made in Europe were artistic rather than commercial successes and gave the following figures:

The Arab brought Ingram larger royalties than any film he had ever made.
Mare Nostrum cost £120,000 and had realised to date £400,000.
The Magician was less successful because of its heavy story, but it doubled its production cost.

The Garden of Allah was estimated at £150,000 by Hollywood, which would probably have meant £200,000. Ingram says he produced it for a trifle over £80,000 which included payments totalling £13,000 against cost of story and scenario, Alice Terry's salary and Ingram's producing fee.

He made the point that with such low production costs more money can be spared for exploitation than in the case of an expensive production like *The Student Prince*.

He made the prophetic statement: 'The film industry is international and I predict that within a few years a thoroughly organised combination of English, French, German, Italian and Swedish producers will make half the yearly output of films saleable throughout the world.' Today the ghost city of Hollywood is a monument to his perspicacity and, ironically, the powerful MGM no longer makes films.

He denied that he was retiring from films. He mentions the illness which he contracted in the desert which led to enforced idleness. He mentions, too, that he has leased his studios to his friend M. Corniglion-Molinier, the head of Franco Film Productions, who wishes him to produce one picture a year and to supervise two. He challenges the claim of Harry Lachman to a major role in the making of *The Garden of Allah*: 'I have never had an assistant whose services were indispensable and whose absence might delay the work of film-production.'

Of the old guard, Seitz, Whytock, de Limur, John George, Rehfeld, Lachman and Powell had gone. Some years in Nice however, were still to be his. Troubled years perhaps, but still years of happiness and achievement. Someone said his initials stood for Rex Imperator; but the uncrowned King of Nice he really was.

Rex with his wife and father at Nice.

11 The Last Films

The management of the Studios was now in the hands of Fred Bacos. Leonce Perret, who leased them for Franco Films, made many films including *Morgane la Sirène* (1927). A pioneer of French films, Perret had made a remarkable *Enfant du Paris* in 1913 and also the popular *Koenigsmark* (1923) with his discovery Ivan Petrovitch, and *Madame sans Gêne* (1925) with Gloria Swanson.

Ingram supervised other productions, *L'Evadée* or *Le Secret de Dhelia* (1928), which was directed by his designer, Henri Menessier, and photographed by Burel. Players included Claire de Lorez, Josyane, Rachel Devirys and Petrovitch. For some time Nice had been growing more important as a film centre. In 1925 L'Herbier shot exteriors for *Le Feu Matthieu Pascal* and *Le Vertige* as did Fescourt for *Les Miserables* and Feuillade for *Stigmate*. Gerard Bourgeois used the Victorine Studios for *L'Homme sans Nerfs* with the German stunt-actor Harry Piel.

In 1926 Feyder shot some scenes for his *Carmen* and Louis Mercanton directed Betty Balfour in *Cinders,* both in Nice. Cavalcanti was shooting *Train sans Yeux,* Perret made *La Femme Nue* with Louise Lagrange, Petrovitch and Nita Naldi. Six films were made at the Victorine including l'Herbier's *Le Diable au Coeur* with Betty Balfour.

1927 saw over thirty films made in the Nice district. At the Victorine seven films were shot including Mercanton's *Croquette* with Betty Balfour, *Sables* by Dmitri Kirsanoff with Nadia Sibirskaia, *Roses of Picardy* by Maurice Elvey, *Confetti* by Graham Cutts, *Bi'cchi* by Jean Durand and *Travelaughs* by Harry Lachman.

In 1928 Constance Talmadge, the American comedienne, arrived with her husband, Captain Alistair Macintosh, and appeared in Mercanton's *Venus* at the Victorine. Six films made in the studio that year included Raymond Bernard's *Tarakanova* with Edith Jehanne, Perret's *Danseuse Orchidée* with Louise Lagrange and Ricardo Cortez. Volkoff's spectacular *Scheherezade* made for the UFA, Berlin, featured Petrovitch, Marcella Albani and Nicolai Koline. This film was also known as *Secrets of the Orient.*

Ingram himself now joined forces with Captain Alistair Macintosh and, with money provided by Ludwig Blattner and a distribution contract with United Artists, planned to make a series of films in his studios. In the *American Theatre Magazine* of January 1928 he deplored the artificiality of American film production and pointed out the advantages of filming in Europe. He expressed his admiration for Griffith's *Intolerance* and Chaplin's *A Woman of Paris* and mentioned the high standard of *Nanook of the North, The Cabinet of Dr Caligari, Chang* and *Potemkin,* only one of which had been filmed in a studio. Again he went on to preach his doctrine of fidelity to environment and of restraint in acting. He justified his claims for Nice as a centre of film-making and foretold that an increasing number of films would be made in Europe for the American market.

That same January he took an action against Newnes & Pearson, publishers of the British magazine *Titbits* who, on the authority of the Continental Press Agency of Paris, had stated that he was retiring from films because of his revulsion against Hollywood, referred to domestic difficulties and to his conversion to Islam. The case was settled out of court on condition that the defendants paid a sum to charity. Ingram declared that he was happily married, had no intention of turning Mohammedan, and that he derived his income from Hollywood.

He continued to enjoy the life of the resort and indulged his hobbies of swimming and boxing. At one of the studio workshops, he devoted himself to sculpture and did some fine African heads and one of his friend Paul Dardé, himself a sculptor.

The death of Vicente Blasco Ibáñez, on 28 January 1928 saddened him. A great funeral at Menton was accompanied by a military escort and represen-tatives of the municipality and local society. In Spain 80,000 people marched to lay wreaths at his birthplace. Some years later, when the republican govern-ment came to power, the body was brought by ship to his home town of Valencia. Ingram travelled with the widow on the ship and it was a moving and emotional scene when the ship docked. Across the coffin was a great flag with the words *The Dead Command,* the title of the great writer's novel.

In the previous September Isadora Duncan met her tragic death when her scarf caught in the axle of the car taking her from Nice to Italy. The last photo of her was taken at the Victorine Studios with Rehba, Rex's Arab dancing girl. Some time previously Isadora attempted suicide by walking into the sea at Nice, but her fur coat kept her afloat and she was ignominiously hauled ashore. The incident led to unwelcome publicity for Rex and speculation about orgies at the studios. She had tried to persuade Rex to film a script of hers. His good looks and intelligence must have marked him as obvious prey for the amorous Isadora, but knowing her erotic capacities he was on his guard. The Bohemian activities of this first flower child were not his style.

In July and August of 1929 the great Russian actor, Ivan Mosjoukine, was appearing in *Der Weisse Teufel* (Tolstoy's *Hadschi Muraad*) his first sound film, which was directed by Alexander Volkoff in Nice. This actor's career had ranged from Czarist Russia to the France of the twenties. He became friendly with the Ingrams and he and Alice used to frequent a local café after their day's work.

Also living in Nice was a young man later to become known as Romain Gary, war hero, diplomat, writer and film director. As he revealed in his book *Promise at Dawn,* he was a son of Mosjoukine from an early romance in that actor's life. Father and son managed to establish friendly relations at this time. Gary was a constant swimmer at the Grande Bleue and planned to swim across the Baie des Anges. He fell in love with a Peruvian girl of fourteen but she had eyes only for the handsome athletic middle-aged man who lazed about on the beach — Rex Ingram.

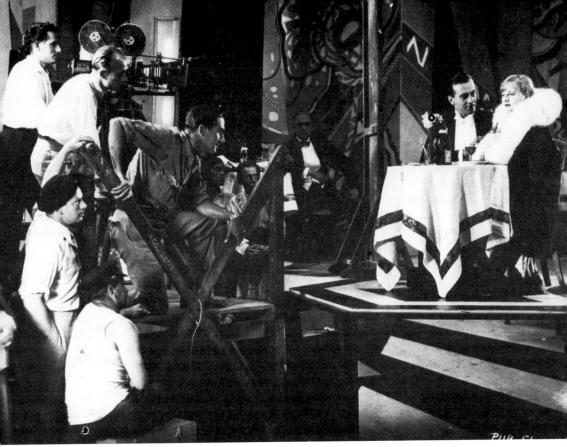

THE THREE PASSIONS, *St George's Productions 1929.* Top: *Ingram directing Alice Terry and Ivan Petrovitch; Burel with head close to camera.*

Bottom: *Getting ready for the ballroom scene.*

For his new film, Cosmo Hamilton, a friend from the early twenties, wrote *The Three Passions,* a story of the jazz generation, of the struggle between capital and labour and of the beneficent influence of religion. A wealthy ship-yard-owner has an unfaithful frivolous wife and a son who serves with a semi-religious community amongst the dock-workers. A pretty young socialite reconciles father and son, a shipyard strike is averted and on his father's death the young man becomes head of the firm. It was a restatement of Fritz Lang's theme from *Metropolis* (1926): *The mediator between the hands and brain must be the heart.*

Menessier designed for this production vast sets of a great industrial plant, dockside scenes, the quiet atmosphere of Oxford and modern domestic interiors. L. H. Burel was the cameraman. He had a remarkable career in the French cinema and was later to become Bresson's favourite cameraman. He was sent to England, France and Germany to do research for Ingram at the script stage. The Oxford scenes were filmed at Magdalen College and the ship-yard scenes, taken at Armstrong's shipyard, Newcastle-on-Tyne, were cut in with the elaborate studio sets at the Victorine.

Alice Terry played the flapper role with her hair dyed blonde, having discarded her famous wig. It was a symbolic gesture as this was her last screen part. Petrovitch played the son and Shayle Gardner, the English actor, gave a fine performance as the rugged industrialist. Claire Eames, wife of Sidney Howard the dramatist, who had played Queen Elizabeth in Marshall Neilan's *Dorothy Vernon of Haddon Hall* with Mary Pickford, acted impressively the role of the selfish dissolute wife. Andrews Engelmann, who had already worked with Ingram, played the repulsive villain. Gerald Fielding, whose family were close friends of the Ingrams, took the part of the gigolo.

For smaller roles and crowd scenes, Ingram drew on his friends and the high society of Nice. Sir Hugo de Bathe (Lily Langtry's husband), Constantine Gries (once Master of Ceremonies to the Czar), Baroness Schomberg, General Markevitch and Prince Gavrousoff lent their presence to the crowd scenes and it is rumoured that Bernard Shaw had a bit role. The etiquette for the banquet scenes was supervised by Earl Haig's butler, Mr Maurice Money.

The film cost $540,000 ($40,000 over budget). One rumour has it that Ludwig Blattner had given Ingram enough money for several films but that he spent it all on the one film. This was expensive, as comparison with costs of First National Pictures will show. Their films averaged $150,000 with $300,000 dollars for specials. Many of Warner's films were made for $50,000. United Artists took the film with no money down, only a guarantee of distribution. The world première took place at Loew's Valencia Theatre, Jamaica, Long Island, on 28 April 1929 and opened in New York the following day at Loew's Metropolitan Theatre.

Ingram had begun the film on 16 May 1928, so it had taken almost a year to make. It had been shot silent, but — as sound had arrived in America — it was also issued with a sound track and a musical score arranged by Hugo Riesenfeld.

The Victorine Studio was equipped for sound and the last silent film made there was Mercanton's *Venus.* Ingram had definite ideas on sound and didn't hesitate to broadcast them. In the London *Evening Standard* of 27 April 1929 he stated: 'Silent Pictures are finished and a good thing too.' He went on to indicate that the cinema had reached an *impasse* and had gone stale. He felt the sound film would gain over the theatre in its use of properly trained actors and improved audibility. Films would be accepted on merit and the star system would disappear. Improvements in sound film-techniques offered a challenge to the creative director who would find new worlds to conquer.

The reception of *The Three Passions* was favourable enough. *La Liberté* of 18 May 1929 spoke of the film's 'powerful impact . . . Intelligent, well-executed and must make the viewers think . . . Alice Terry is particularly distinguished, always young and beautiful as she is. Andrews Engelmann is effortlessly impressive in the style of von Stroheim, the man you love to hate'. *La Soir* of 19 May 1929 said: 'The direction of Ingram is, as always, sumptuous and powerful. The details are evocative to a supreme degree and the camera-angles reveal astonishing technique.'

At this time George Bernard Shaw was a frequent visitor to the Ingrams and Rex was interested in filming *Arms and the Man* but Shaw would not give him the rights. This peeved Rex, who replied that he was only interested in the Oscar Strauss musical version – *The Chocolate Soldier*.

The young Grace Moore, then starting her career as a singer, was another acquaintance and Mary Garden, the famous opera singer who appeared in *Thaïs* for Universal when Rex was working there, was a close friend.

Gladys Cooper, too, was a constant visitor at the studios and strangest of all was the meeting of Ingram with an up-and-coming young British director, Alfred Hitchcock. Ingram very kindly took him aside and told him that he should do what he had done and have his name changed. 'You'll never get any-where with a name like that,' said Rex. Surely the most ironic remark in film history.

Rex's father and brother visited Nice around this period and it was the first time all three were re-united since Rex left Ireland in 1911. Rex's father actually advised on ecclesiastical details of *The Three Passions*.

The coming months were to be an anxious time. Ingram had to raise money for future productions. In November of 1929 he went to London for the first time in five years. It was rumoured that he was to make a film for Lord Beaverbrook but nothing came of it.

Ivan Petrovich had left the Ingram studios after appearing in three of his films. His new career brought him to Germany where he became quite a popular player. In more recent years he played in Pabst's *Der Process* (1947) and Louis Malle's *L'Ascenseur Pour L'Echafaud* (1957). He died in 1962.

Alice Terry at last decided to retire from films. She didn't like the new demands made on the actor by the sound film. She revolted against the constant need to control her weight. She was just not prepared to sacrifice herself to a career in films. So without any heartbreak she decided to make her exit. It was certainly not due to the lack of an expressive voice, for the one she had was most pleasant to hear. Had she continued to play in films, she might have developed as a comedienne. It remains regrettable that she never appeared in a sound film.

Ingram, however, still had the problems of the sound film to handle. At this difficult time he found the studios taken out of his control. Through the manipulations of Edouard Corniglion-Molinier their ownership passed to

THE THREE PASSIONS, *St George's Productions 1929, Claire Eames and Shayle Gardner.*

Franco Film in which Corniglion-Molinier had more than an interest. Ingram was furious. Apart from losing his own chances of control of the studios, they were sold to Franco Film for a sum which did not make allowance for all the improvements Ingram had undertaken. Ingram immediately brought an action against Corniglion-Molinier for fraud before the Nice courts on 30 October 1930. This was a sensational case but curiously it seems to have received very little mention in the local papers. Corniglion-Molinier was a powerful personage and a tough opponent to handle. In addition to being a prominent lawyer and film financier, he had become a captain aviator of the reserve, which function was to bring him some considerable fame in years to come.

Ingram lost his case which he was unable to prove, and was ordered to pay costs. With a savage tenacity he appealed the case to the Aix Court of Appeal. He now accused his studio manager, Fred Bacos, of having stolen papers from his office which would prove the guilt of Corniglion-Molinier. The appeal dragged on into 1936 when Ingram again lost his case and was ordered to pay

THE THREE PASSIONS, *St George's Productions 1929. After the ball.*

costs which must now have been considerable. However, by this time Ingram had left his beloved Victorine Studios and had shaken the dust of France from his feet, to take up residence in North Africa.

With this troubled background and still using the Victorine Studios, Ingram embarked on the production of his first sound film. There had been much negotiation with British film financiers. William Hutter of the Duke of York's Theatre was reputed to be Ingram's backer for a film to be made largely in North Africa which would receive distribution by United Artists. But although finance was guaranteed, in reality the production lived from hand to mouth. From time to time various backers were brought in, including the English Mr Mansfield Markham.

The new film *Baroud* was duly announced in June 1931. It was to be made in North Africa, Nice and London with Alexandre D'Arcy in the lead. The heroine was to be an unknown. The previous year, it had been announced that Ingram was to make a film in London with Alice Terry and a London actor in

THE THREE PASSIONS, *St George's Productions 1929. The shipping magnate's office.*

the leads.

The plot of *Baroud* was based on a story devised by Rex Ingram and Benno Vignay, whose novel *Amy Jolly* later provided the material for von Sternberg's *Morocco*. The question of a leading man proved difficult and Ingram decided to play the part himself. The leading feminine role was entrusted to Rosita Garcia, who, under the name of Rosita Ramirez, appeared in Ingram's films in small parts from the time of *Where the Pavement Ends*. Her performance in *Baroud* was not particularly distinguished. She appeared in some films afterwards, including Fairbanks' *The Private Life of Don Juan* for Korda, before fading from the screen.

It was announced that Ingram was to make French, Spanish and Arab versions of the film, but in fact only the English and French versions were made. For the latter, Ingram's part was taken by Roland Caillaux and the heroine was played by Colette Darfeuil.

Ingram seemed to be making this, his first talkie, as difficult as possible. He undertook the lead and assembled as motley a group of players as ever took part in one film. The varying range of accents militated against any sort of vocal unity. The heroine's nurse was played by Arabella Fields, a portly negro actress from Philadelphia who had acted on the stage in Holland and Russia. The part of the heroine's father was taken by an Italian businessman, Signor Moretti, who used the screen name of Felipe Montes, and that of the villain by Andrews Engelmann, a white Russian. Pierre Batcheff played the hero's friend. The confusion of tongues did not help the film, but mercifully it had not a great deal of dialogue and relied more on its scenes of action and evocation of local atmosphere.

The film took a year to prepare and a year to make. It cost 22 million francs or $1 million. It was released in France by Armor Films and in Great Britain by Ideal Films Ltd. The British trade presentation took place on 28 September 1932 at the Prince Edward Theatre in Ingram's presence. It was not too well received and before the final credits reached the screen the projectionist had drawn the curtains, a rather humiliating gesture towards its maker. Its British release on 27 February 1933 was followed by its American première at the Mayfair Theatre, New York, on 18 March.

Baroud, a story of love and tribal war amongst the Berber tribes in the Atlas Mountains of Morocco (in America the film was called *Love in Morocco*), is not a successful film. On the other hand it is by no means a dull one. Visually it is one of the most beautiful films to reach the screen with exciting battles and Arab horseriding, as well as scenes which reflect the very spirit of Morocco.

George Wakhevitch, the distinguished designer of theatre and film has given us a most interesting insight into the work of Ingram at this time in his autobiography of 1977, *L'Envers des Decors*. He was the young assistant of the equally young Jean Lafitte, engaged by Ingram to design *Baroud* which he proposed to make in 1931. He speaks of the months of preparation of the designs, plans, details of architecture and furnishings. 'Before shooting,' he says, 'Rex Ingram worked out his production with models and voluminous sketches for the decors. As he had been all through his career in Hollywood he was well organised and had a horror of improvisation. This was an excellent approach but not much used in Europe.'

In the winter of 1930 the workshops were preparing the sets. It was one of the first French films to be also made in an English version. In the grounds of the Victorine Ingram had a replica of the great casbah of Telouet. The designer's bible was the book by Albert Laprade on the gardens and houses of Morocco. A member of El Glaoui's household came from Marrakesh to advise on detail and the designers were supplied with many photos and documents, although they would have preferred to travel to North Africa to study the life and customs of the Arab people. John Birkel who constructed the sets taught the two young designers. Lafitte and Wakhevitch, the secrets of his trade — how frail exterior settings could be made to resist wind and weather and how paint could be given permanence.

Wakhevitch goes on to say: 'As he played in the English version of *Baroud* Rex Ingram was never satisfied with his acting. Because of this we were ordered not to strike the set on stage two which represented the quarters of the sub-officers. Here once or twice a week he would repeat the scene with Pierre Batcheff, a star of the period.' This young man of Russian origin had a most beautiful face and was very cultured — an excellent jeune premier of the thirties. He had begun his career with George Pitoeff in Geneva but from 1924 had played in films by Gance, l'Herbier, Bernard, Cavalcanti, Clair, and in Bunuel and Dali's *Chien Andalou.* His tragic suicide in April 1932 just after *Baroud* was a loss to the French cinema. He was a brother-in-law of Jacques Doniol-Valcroze, film critic and founder of *Les Cahiers du Cinema.*

Ewart Hodgson in the London *Daily Express* gave it three stars out of five and felt it was scenically good but dramatically weak. G. A. Atkinson waxed enthusiastic over it. 'There are long sequences in *Baroud* in which Ingram captures the stealthy fascination exerted by the great silent films such as *Robin Hood* or his own *The Four Horsemen* . . . Its flow of beautiful open-air pictures revives one's faith in the screen medium and there is rich food for the romanticist in these skilfully composed scenes of Moroccan landscapes and white-walled towns in which the quality of the sunlight is so vivid that the shadows are translucent . . .

'*Baroud* is entertainment in the screen's best tradition but it is also the work of a great artist, and there is room for great artists in a profession crowded with mediocrities.'

The *New York Times* of 20 March 1933 wrote: 'It is an unusual entertainment, pleasantly amateurish in its acting, juvenile in its story development and definitely charming in its recreation of the Moroccan atmosphere and the dark beauty of its people as idealised by Mr Ingram's canvas. The pastel skies, the mountains and the desert country, the narrow winding alleys of Marrakesh, the flat white houses and the Moorish civilisation make a fascinating background. The picture is flooded with picturesque types, Spahis, African serving women, beggars, dancing girls, bandits from the desert and sinister Europeans.'

Ingram's own performance is rather stilted and a little ill at ease. A trace of Irish accent still remains. He was not helped by some incredible dialogue of the 'Gee, baby' type. However, Clarence Brown was so impressed by his performance that he offered him a Hollywood contract to play in his films, and, who knows, but he may have had him in mind for a lead opposite Garbo. But Ingram was not interested.

Opposite: *Bernard Shaw and the Ingrams* (top); *the son of El Glaoui, Rex Ingram, Rosita Garcia and Alice Terry* (bottom).

Le Fils du Pacha. (Maroc)

الحاج سيد محمد نقر الدين

RexIngram

جرا نعام

Above: *Rex and his young friend Johanna Busby.* **Opposite:** *Ingram the pious Mohammedan.*

As a sound film, *Baroud* has some points of technical interest. Its quite successful open air sound recording was rather rare at a time when films were inclined to be boxed-in studio theatre. Its music-track by Louis Levy was excellent, with exciting theme music sung also as a song, 'Le Cafard', ('The Cockroach') by Laura Salerni in Dietrich-like manner in the café scene. This song was composed by Arthur Young.

The most striking appearance was that of Andrews Engelmann as the treacherous Si Amarok. This actor continued to play in German films throughout the war and ended up pursuing a commercial career in Switzerland.

Burel, the cameraman, recalls in a letter to the author: 'When he (Ingram) was preparing *Baroud*, we went to Morocco for four weeks in order to see everything. He was so conscientious that he made the journey from Tangiers to Rabat in cars used by lower-class Moroccans. At Rabat he donned an Arab costume so that he could more intimately mingle with the street crowds without being identified as a European. Together we made a long journey on

BAROUD, *Ingram Productions 1932. Andrews Engelmann as Si Amorok.*

Opposite: *An African sketch, 1932.*

horse-back into the High Atlas which had not at that time been completely pacified, in order to visit the casbahs of the Glaoui and those most distant and isolated in the mountains.' Burel's image of Ingram at this time is worth recording. 'As a man, Rex was a very agreeable friend of large and generous ideas. It was he who organised at the Studios a free canteen for the workers which operated all day and where they could obtain sandwiches, patés, fruit, beer, tea, coffee and minerals. A sober person himself, he did not object to his friends drinking, so long as they didn't abuse it. He had a horror of drunkards.

'Every year at Christmas he dressed in the studio a splendid Christmas tree and all the workers and their children collected toys, clothes, pipes and quantities of all sorts of things often of some value.

'To sum up he was a very good artist, very cultivated, well informed and dignified.'

For the visit to the Atlas Mountains the safe conduct issued by General Catroux on 11 July 1931 authorised Ingram and two companions to proceed

An African sketch, 1932.

to Telouet, Ouarzazat and Quarzazat. They were guaranteed the protection of the French army, but if they went beyond these points they would do so at their own risk.

It is clear that Ingram steeped himself in the atmosphere of Morocco and got to know the country and its people intimately. El Glaoui, the great feudal despot of the Atlas, a man steeped in blood and ambition, torn between his heritage of rapine and the softer ways of Western culture was an ally of the French and was regarded by a later generation of independence fighters as a traitor to his country. However he and Ingram got on well and El Glaoui helped the *Baroud* production in many ways, lending swords, guns and costumes as Ingram required them. He also entertained Ingram and Rosita Garcia at his palace at Marrakesh. El Glaoui's stronghold was at Telouet in the Atlas Mountains, and Ingram called his chief in *Baroud* Caid of Ilouet.

Another influential friend of Ingram was General Juin, an important figure in the life of Morocco.

Now the old story of Ingram's conversion to Mohammedanism once more came into the news, and this time there seems to have been something to it. Gabriel Costa, who worked as a press agent for Ingram, wrote an article for the *Film Pictorial* (London) on 15 October 1932. In it he mentions Ingram's adoption of the Islamic faith and that he was received by Abdul Medjid, ex-Sultan of Turkey and Caliph of All Islam. This sounded like a tall Ingram yarn so I asked his friend, Max de Vaucorbeil, for his opinion. He thinks that, in fact, he did become a Mohammedan during one of his Moroccan visits. He used to sign his name as Bin Aliq Nasr El-Din which means in Arabic, The Son of the Union of Victory and Religion.

Perhaps a tribute Ingram appreciated more than any other was that from no less a person than Le Maréchal Lyautey in a letter from Paris dated 23 March 1933. 'Je vous addresse avec plaisir ma photographie dedicacée et je vous félicite a nouveau de votre belle oeuvre qui fera mieux connaitre au public le vrai visage de l'Empire Cherifien.'

From his residence in Nice at the Villa Binh Hoa, St Maurice, Ingram announced another film to be made in North Africa with Rosita Garcia — *Simoun,* but this never materialised. The big lawsuit over the studio was still unsettled. The glorious adventure was drawing to a close.

In Ingram's mind the villain of the piece was Corniglion-Molinier, who in later years had an extraordinary career. As a film producer, he launched *Courrier Sud* (1936), *Drôle de Drame* (1937) and *Espoir* (1939), the latter directed by André Malraux in Spain. He had experience of flying in Spain and on the outbreak of World War II he became commander of the Free French Aerial Forces. On the defeat of Germany he was appointed a senator, then a deputy holding several ministries, including that of Ministry for Justice. He died in 1962.

From its beginning in 1918-20 the Victorine Studios were associated with many famous films. Robert Boudrioz's *L'Atre,* a film of great distinction was the first to be made there. Léon Poirier's *Geneviève* appeared in 1923. Then there were the Ingram films. Since his time landmarks of the cinema have poured from the studios which at one stage came under the control of the municipality of Nice. Gance made his *Venus Aveuglée* here, Marcel Carné

Visiteurs du Soir and *Les Enfants du Paradis,* Jean Gremillon *Lumière d'Eté,* Delannoy *L'Eternal Retour,* Tati *Mon Oncle,* Clement *Les Jeux Interdits,* Ophuls *Lola Montez,* Peter Ustinov *Lady L* and Vadim *Et Dieu Créa la Femme.* A very honourable record indeed.

For the remainder of Ingram's time in Nice there was much speculation, many projects, but for him it was the end of a chapter and a time for decision.

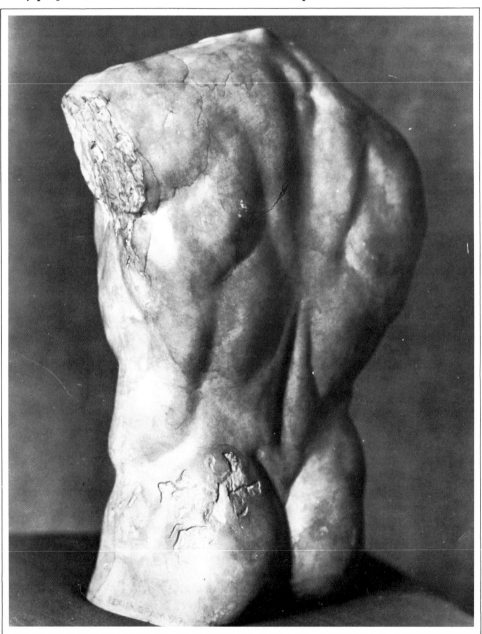

Torso by Ingram.

12 The Last Years

Early in 1934 Rex and Alice paid a short visit to Cairo, and in May of the same year he said farewell to Nice and returned to Cairo as a permanent base. His collection of Arab art was deposited with the Cairo Museum. Alice, however, returned to Hollywood where her mother had died. She remained there until Rex joined her two years later. He spent those years wandering in North Africa and writing his novel *The Legion Advances,* a violent and colourful tale of Arab life dedicated to Marechal Lyautey, with whom he had been in correspondence since the time of *Baroud.*

On 17 March 1936 he returned to the United States and settled down with Alice at 501 North Irving Boulevard, Hollywood. John Seitz met him and found him little changed except for high blood-pressure, caused by an illness contracted in Egypt.

The Ingrams moved into the San Fernando Valley where they had two adjacent bungalow houses, one of which was used as a living quarters and the other as Rex's private refuge to which he could escape from visitors and carry on his writing and sculpture. This was to be the couple's final home, except for a period when it was rented to Clark Gable and when Rex was off on one of his Mexican expeditions. When Gable married Carole Lombard, the house was put up for sale and the Ingrams returned to a former residence at 2041 Pinehurse Road. The sale fell through, however, and they returned to the San Fernando Valley houses.

In 1939 his novel *Mars in the House of Death,* with illustration by Carlos Ruano Llopis, made its appearance. It was a melodramatic story of a bullfighter and his love affairs. It was uneven in quality with some good writing. It had all the elements of popular film material and was reminiscent of Blasco Ibáñez's *Blood and Sand.* The *New York Times* reviewer went so far as to say, 'It was integrated by a keen intelligence. One or two of these sequences are worthy of any novelist living. They give you to understand why, in the history of the moving pictures, Rex Ingram belongs with the early immortals.' To boost the book Rex made several public appearances. He also wrote some short stories and in 1940 made a trip to Hawaii and then back to Mexico.

With the coming of war he wanted to enlist, but his high blood-pressure ruled this out and he reluctantly deferred to medical opinion. But he did place his unique knowledge of the Arab world at the disposal of the Washington authorities.

He had never really liked the talkies and he had lost interest in film-making. On a visit, his old colleague Whytock found him with a pile of film scripts sent to him by his friend Eddie Mannix, now vice-president of MGM. He felt

Left: *African head by Ingra*

Right: *Head of a Jester (Shorty Ben Mairech)*
by Ingram.

that Mannix could get forty directors to do any of these scripts, but that there just might be the one script that only he could do. When he found that, he would consider directing again. He had always been choosy about what he wanted to film.

About 1942 he heard that Paramount was going to make *For Whom the Bell Tolls* by Hemingway and this interested him. Seitz, then working with Paramount, had a chat with Buddy de Sylva about it but as Rex had been out of films for ten years, they felt the risk was too great. The news did not seem to perturb him.

Old friends looked him up and he surveyed the Hollywood scene in its new manifestations. Erich von Stroheim and Denise Vernac visited him. He watched the successful work of John Ford who was a friend of his. 'This fellow Ford has a very good sense of texture,' he said, adding 'and he didn't even attend an art school.' Amongst the other people who remembered and admired him was David Selznick who remade two of his films.

When Rex left Egypt he had left behind his furnishings and belongings. Wartime difficulties prevented him from sending for his precious collection from the Cairo Museum. He planned to return and reclaim his treasures and en route see his father and brother once more. To his ageing father Rex had always been a good son in spite of differences of opinion. He was also much attached to his brother, whom he sent to Davos for recuperation after World War I.

On 27 May 1947 he wrote:

My dear Clere
        I got your three letters about the O.M. The last one undated came this morning. The first a few weeks ago, when I was at Laguna Beach, a sea resort not more than two hundred miles from here. Alice read it over to me on the phone and I told her to wire some money to Tolleshunt Knights in case Daddie had immediate need of a nurse and to cable him to cable back if he had need of anything. Naturally a man can't go on living the way the O.M. has done for forty years — tramping four or five miles a day — for ever. You say the doctor finds him breaking up. Well that's only to be expected. They might be able to shoot hormones into him and rejuvenate him for a while, but I doubt if the English doctors have them. I wrote him enclosing a letter for you from Laguna, telling him to get a nurse if necessary, and in any case a locum tenens, as he did in Ireland when illness or absence obliged him to get someone to take his place. I suppose he has had one during the last two or three weeks? How much does he have to pay a neighbouring cleric to come over on Sundays and take his services for him? And how about the parish? Does someone else have to go around visiting the parishioners keeping up their morale (Christian morale naturally)? You know from time to time I send him a little money, but I have an idea that, like the clothes I send him, he saves it! In fact some months ago he let it out in a letter that he was trying to put something aside to leave you, as he was afraid you'd find it hard to make ends meet on your army pension. He is damn lucky to have Mrs Hines to look after him, and apparently her children keep him in a happy

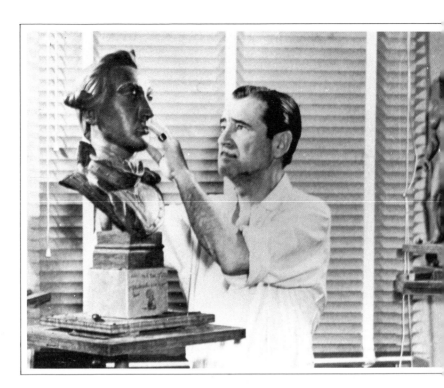

Top: *Ingram at work on a head of his ancestor, the Chevalier de Johnston.*
Bottom: *Ingram in his Hollywood home.*

mood, though he wrote that he was afraid one of them had contracted T.B. As this is only the 21st May, I'm sending this letter to Beaconsfield Five. Airmail should not take more than three days to reach you. When you write let me know whether to write to you to the same address or to Osborne House. I know that you must feel disappointed at having to quit the Army before you had counted, but frankly, seeing that your physical condition prevented you from taking over an active command during the last war, I think you're better out of it. I am sure that you should be back at your writing, and I've no doubt that you'll be at it again and make it a profitable profession as time goes on. Only last week I was at the home of a damn nice fellow — an old soldier of the First World War and a nut on horses — and found a copy of *Saddle Up* on his bookshelves, which are filled with books on horses. Without telling him you were my brother, I asked him what he thought of it. He replied very Britishly 'Top Hole'. Now if you need anything for yourself as well as for the O.M. write me. I expect I'll be on my way to Egypt in the next couple of months as all my personal belongings are there, you remember. I think I loaned my art collection to the Egyptian Government and thank God the Huns didn't get to Cairo so it's still there. But I must go there to get it sent here, and supervise the packing and shipping. I will do my best to see the old man. Maybe this time he'll be well enough to come over to Ireland, as I must go there, having been away since 1911. Maybe the three of us could meet in Dublin. However all that depends on how long this Egyptian business will take me. I hope the food shipments are reaching you regularly. Let me have your news as soon as you get to Osborne.

All for now
Love
Rex

P.S. Ask the O.M.'s doctor what he thinks about giving him a few shots of hormones. If he likes the idea I can airmail a supply of the Serum. R.I.

On 24 July 1947 he left New York on the Cunard liner *Vasconia* for Liverpool where he docked on the evening of 5 August. Next day he was meeting his brother at Euston Station, London. He visited his father at Tolleshunt Knights, and also met his old school friend Colonel Roderick Greer who says: 'I never expected to see my boyhood hero again. I had a wonderful meeting with him in London in 1947 soon after I had been demobilised. His brother, Colonel Hitchcock, was announced one day as waiting to see me in my office in Pall Mall. A moment or two later the door opened and standing there in fighting pose was Rex Ingram. It was a joyous reunion and although naturally he had changed over the years, having lost his fine athletic appearance, he was still the same kindly character that I had always known him to be. At that time he was on the way to see his father, who was still running a parish, even though a very old man by this time. From there he went to North Africa again and expressed the hope that he might see me again on his way back to America, some months later. However that was my last meeting with him and the last I heard of him was that he died in Hollywood.'

After a week in London he travelled to Egypt on the P. & O. troop ship *Arundel Castle*. At Malta he fell ill and was looked after by Colonel R. R. Evans, a friend of his brother. In Egypt there was much to do, as some of his things had found their way to King Farouk's palace, from which they were promptly recovered. There were places and friends to visit and on 12 February he was meeting the Sultan of Morocco, Sidi Mohammed, and his Grand Chamberlain, Si Mameri. The following day he lunched with General Juin. He was staying at the Hotel Balima in Rabat. From there he moved to the El Minzah Palace, Tangier. He wrote to his brother on various topics, including American politics, and suggested that General MacArthur should be proposed for president. He left Tangier on 1 March and stayed at the Bristol Hotel, Gibraltar. Here he met Colonel Brickman, a friend of his brother, who was about to depart for the Gold Coast to settle some unrest there. He visited La Mesquita in Cordova, Ronda, Seville and Malaga and sailed on the *M/s Sobieski* for New York on 15 March from Cadiz. He had suffered heart attacks in Tangier and Seville and was given a palliative, escilarina, of which he took seventy-five drops a day. From New York, he travelled to California by train.

He spent some time organising his home and added new rooms to the building to accommodate his collection.

On 6 May 1948 he was made an honorary member of the Screen Director's Guild. The nomination was signed by George Marshall.

Restless as ever, he then set out for Haiti, Cuba and Vera Cruz. His old friend from Nice, Max de Vaucorbeil, who was making a film in Haiti, met him there but found him aged and suffering from a high blood pressure against which he had to take precautions. It was nevertheless a happy meeting and they had much to discuss about the old days in Nice. While in Vera Cruz he contracted malaria and was confined to bed in Mazatlan for several weeks.

Alice Terry continues the story: 'When he came back to Hollywood he was very thin and looked sick, but soon started to gain weight and was very interested in a book by Ralph Korngold — *Citizen Toussaint* (Eisenstein had been attracted to the same subject). He thought it would make a very exciting film and talked about writing a script but he was still under the doctor's care and his blood pressure was high. He was to have some X-rays made and the doctor thought it would be easier if he stayed in the hospital while they were being made. He was highly nervous and this would be easier for him than going by car, each day. I went to see him twice a day and on 21 July I sat with him for an hour or two and he felt fine. He was to come to a clinic in the Valley the next day for some heart tests, so I made arrangements to pick him up at nine the next morning. My birthday was 24 July and he told me to pick out something nice for myself from him and said, 'I will see you in the morning. Be sure and get something pretty.' I left and shopped for an hour and when I got home the telephone was ringing. It was the hospital, and the doctor asked me to come immediately, that Rex was unconscious. When I got back to the hospital (Park View Hospital) twenty minutes later, he was in a coma and passed away a short time after.'

Rex was cremated and the funeral service was held at Glendale in the 'Wee Kirk o' the Heather', Forest Lawn, on 26 July 1950. The celebrant was the Reverend Mr John C. Donnell, Rector of the Church of Our Saviour, Los

Angeles. Among those at the funeral were Ramon Novarro, Mrs Jerry Croft, Mrs Robert Ames, Constance Talmadge, Claire du Brey, Antonio Moreno, Gilbert Roland, Bette Davis, John Seitz, Grant Whytock, John and Mrs Batten.

His death was recorded in the world press. For Alice Terry it was a grievous loss. This handsome talented Irishman had responded to her spirit and had been her close companion for nearly thirty years. He had developed her innate talents and made her one of the first ladies of the screen.

Fortunately, unlike so many other pioneers of the cinema, he was able to leave his wife comfortably off. His house and valuable collection of *objets d'art* went to her as well as $200,000. A trust fund was set up to be divided between his father and brother on the death of Alice.

But his father died on 10 April 1951, less than a year after. His brother Clere, otherwise Lt Colonel F. C. Hitchcock, OBE, MC, lived on for a little over a decade. He received his first decoration in World War I and spent some time in Davos recovering from wounds. He served in the Indian Army. An expert on horses, boxing and military history, he wrote three books: *Stand To*, a diary of life in the trenches, *To Horse* and *Saddle Up*, two classic books on horse-riding. His son Rex carried on the army tradition.

Of the other figures in the Ingram story, Robert Hichens died a day before Rex. Lee Lawrie died on 21 January 1965. Ramon Novarro. before his tragic and brutal murder on 31 October 1968, had more or less retired from the screen, occasionally appearing in films and television character parts. His speculation in real estate left him a wealthy man and amongst the hobbies of his later years painting played a large part. John Seitz added to his honours with films like *Double Indemnity, The Lost Weekend, Sunset Boulevard* and the Preston Sturges films, *Sullivan's Travels, The Miracle of Morgan's Creek* and *Hail the Conquering Hero*. He died at the Motion Picture and TV Hospital, Woodland Hills, California on 27 February 1979 at the age of eighty-six years. Grant Whytock is still editing films and Willis Goldbeck is a producer of films, including those of John Ford.

Today Alice Terry lives in retirement in her home in San Fernando Valley. Her elder sister Edna shares the house with her and has encouraged her graceful talent as a painter. In spite of the encroachment of industrialisation into the valley, the house retains its rural aspect while inside the sculptures of Rex and his paintings by Dinet, Horace Vernet, Guillaumet and William Etty fill the rooms.

When, in 1951, Columbia made *Valentino,* covering events which closely touched her life, she successfully sued the company for $75,000 on the grounds that the film represented her as having an affaire with Valentino, before and after her marriage to Rex. The film was not a success at any level, particularly on that of truth. Even more peculiar was the *Valentino* of Ken Russell in 1977. The use of a Slav dancer to play the great Latin lover was typical of Russell's flight from reality although Nureyev gave a very good performance. But when Russell himself undertook the role of Rex Ingram the last pretence of fidelity to fact was abandoned and in the scenes where Ingram is shown directing *The Four Horsemen of the Apocalypse* travesty is scarcely too strong a word.

In 1961 Vincente Minnelli made an updated version of *The Four Horsemen of the Apocalypse* set in World War Two with Glenn Ford and Ingrid Thulin in the leads. It was a complete failure because the whole spirit of the Blasco Ibáñez book, so skilfully captured by Ingram, had vanished, leaving instead a cold, technically adequate substitution.

Painting has given Alice a new source of creative activity, which she finds most congenial. She finds it easier to assess her work as a painter. She confessed to finding the varying opinions of others confusing to her as an actress. 'If you are conceited, you believe the ones that like you. If not, you are completely thrown.'

At seventy-four I found her a witty, charming and completely modest woman with a beautiful expressive voice that belied her age. There was an incredible youthfulness about her as she amusingly reminisced: 'Well, I do think you have to keep a sense of humour, and if you don't do that, I think you are lost, and I think it is this that helped me through the early years, because everything was not too serious to me. Yes, I used to worry about things, but it didn't kill me if I didn't get any place. I thought: 'Well, I'm an actress, Sue me.'

I was particularly interested in her reaction to my biography of her husband. She said: 'I think you know Rex. It seems strange that you know him so well without ever having met him, but there were things that I didn't understand about him that you didn't understand either. I never did quite understand Rex, but I think that was why I was in love with him. I think the minute you begin to understand somebody you've had it.'

Shakespeare's Katherina would have approved of the wifely tact displayed in the following story by Alice: 'There was a quiz book which tested your good taste by providing things to choose. So I picked them out and Rex had picked them out before, and he came to me after I'd won and said 'I don't understand, because your taste is not as good as mine. How do you do it?' and I said, 'I picked out what I thought *you'd* like.' He said 'I give up with you.'

Today Rex's old studios at the Victorine in Nice operate in spite of rumours of destruction. The Villa Rex still carries his name and has had many residents, including the distinguished young artist Raymond Moretti, installed there by the municipality of Nice. As I write, Terence Young of the James Bond films is in residence with plans for continuing the work of the studios. They have been enlarged since Rex's day, but the basic pattern is still there and you can see the tank where the under-water scenes were done for *Mare Nostrum*. Even some of the old hands like Amleto Negri still work there and recall the great days of Ingram. The achievements of the studios have been celebrated some years ago in a film made for French television, *Les Victoires de la Victorine*, produced by Mario Beunat and René Predal and directed by Antoine Leonard.

It is doubtful if Ingram would recognise the Hollywood of today. Television has hit the film industry hard. MGM has disappeared, its costumes and props auctioned off. Before his death Louis B. Mayer was to taste the defeat of being driven out of the studio he ruled like an oriental potentate. Some of the old studios still stand, but change has come and, like Rex prophesied, many American films are now made in Europe. But the cinema has a capacity for survival and keeps coming up for air in the most unexpected places. In spite of the concentration on technical dexterity and monster productions the medium will always be served by the individual artist such as Ingram always was.

Few film-makers of the past considered their work to be of any permanent value. 'Writing on sand', Griffith called it. But, in spite of great destruction of films in the past, much has been preserved, thanks to the emergence of film archives all over the world in 1935, which set out to preserve films of artistic, scientific and historic value. Even films believed to have been destroyed have a habit of turning up in the strangest places. Many Ingram films which were believed lost have been found.

Ingram's name was kept alive by *The Four Horsemen of the Apocalypse* largely, it must be admitted, because of its association with Valentino. This has been widely shown by film archives and film clubs all over the world. Copies of his other films are deposited in many of those archives. For instance the only known copy of *The Arab* was shown to me by the late Myrtil Frida in the Czech Film Archive in Prague and several of his films are preserved in the Moscow Film Archives. It was directly as a result of research for this book that I came across the negative of *Baroud,* which has a special interest as being Ingram's only sound film and one in which he himself appears. It is now deposited in the National Film Archive in London. The early films he made for Universal are not known to exist anywhere, but a fragment of one of them was found in Dublin. The short films which he scripted or acted in for Edison, Vitagraph and Fox are probably in archives whose entire holdings have yet to be catalogued. One such film, the Vitagraph *Upper Hand,* is held in the National Film Archive in London. In a Robertson-Cole/FBO film of 1923, *Mary of the Movies,* Rex appears briefly as himself, directing a film.

Some biographical confusion arose when a black actor named Rex Ingram achieved prominence in *Green Pastures* (1936) and *The Thief of Bagdad* (1940) and invariably facts are transposed in the film books in listing the activities of the two Rex Ingrams. One wonders if the black player deliberately chose his name in honour of the great Irish director.

Ingram was a great film maker. Even if he did not reach the greatest heights, it is something that his aspirations took him in that direction. The body of work he gave to the cinema provided millions of filmgoers with considerable pleasure and he influenced the industry by setting standards of presentation which have come to be those accepted today. He helped to establish the primacy of the screen image, bringing to it his flair for composition and design and subtleties of photographic light and shade. He used great cameramen like John Seitz, Lee Garmes and L. H. Burel. While he may not have invented the grammar of the film, he used its devices with taste and intelligence. His love of and appreciation of the cinema made him aware of all contemporary achievements, and he was one of the first to acclaim the work of people like Flaherty and Eisenstein. He was passionately devoted to his craft, was a great director of actors, and had a sure instinct for developing their potentialities. Valentino, Novarro, Alice Terry, Lewis Stone, Barbara La Marr, Antonio Moreno and Ivan Petrovitch were household words in the twenties. They were all Ingram people and the majority were his discoveries. Many of his prophecies were to come true. In his thinking, he was far ahead of his time, and he predicted the drift away from the front-office controls of Hollywood. His launching of the Nice studios showed his independent turn of mind and his courage in facing up to a challenge. While he was regarded as the great romantic of the screen, he still brought considerable realism to his work, a quality praised by von Stroheim. He strove for fidelity to background and environment, used natural types, and stamped his work with the mark of truth. His break into cinema was reminiscent of the young Orson Welles, for Rex directed his first film from his own script at the early age of twenty-three. He was only twenty-seven when he made the memorable *Four Horsemen of the Apocalypse*. With his four great films *The Four Horsemen of the Apocalypse*, *The Conquering Power*, *Scaramouche* and *Mare Nostrum*, he earns a niche in film history. If his efforts did not always achieve success, it was perhaps due to that 'dram of eale˙ that doubts the whole substance'. In that he was essentially human, and it is as a warm human being most of his friends like to remember him.

A painting by Alice Terry.

Filmography

ABBREVIATIONS:

ad: art direction
asst ph: assistant photographer
at: art titles
asst d: assistant director
d: director

ed: editor
lp: leading players
mus d: musical director
ph: photography
p: producer

pc: production company
prod man: production manager
sc: scenario
st: story
tech assts: technical assistants

1 The films for Universal

THE GREAT PROBLEM (1916)

pc: Universal — Bluebird Photoplays Inc
dir, sc and st: Rex Ingram
lp: *Violet Mersereau (Mary Carson and Peggy),
Dan Hanlon (Bill Carson), Lionel Adams (George
Devereaux), Kittens Reichert (Peggy the child),
William J. Dyer (Skinny McGee), Mrs J. J.
Brundage (Mrs Devereaux), Howard Crampton
(Joseph), Nellie Slattery (Housekeeper), Lou
Sterns (James Carlton).*
Released: USA 17.4.16
Length: five reels
English title: *Truth*

Bill Carson is condemned to twelve years
imprisonment for housebreaking and, when his
wife dies of shock, his daughter Peggy is left to
the care of his pal Skinny McGee. Carson swears
vengeance against George Devereaux, the
prosecuting attorney who secured his conviction.
On the death of McGee, Peggy becomes a pick-
pocket. Meanwhile, in the boardroom of a reform
organisation, George Devereaux undertakes to
prove that a criminal can be cured by the
influence of better surroundings and when Peggy
is arrested she is chosen for the experiment. For
two years Peggy lives at Devereaux's home and
changes her old habits and is to be married to a
charming young man. At the church, however,
she realises she loves Devereaux and refuses to go
through with the ceremony. She flees from the
Devereaux home and takes up her old career of
crime.

Carson, released from jail, waylays Devereaux
outside his home with the intention of shooting
him. Peggy arrives on the scene, sizes up the
situation and receives the bullet intended for her
patron. But she does not die, her father reforms
and Devereaux realises the outcome of all this
must be marriage with Peggy.

BROKEN FETTERS (1916)

pc: Universal-Bluebird Photoplays Inc
dir and sc: Rex Ingram
ph: B. C. (Duke) Hayward
lp: *Kittens Reichert (Mignon as a child), Violet
Mersereau (Mignon grown up), Charles Francis
(Kong Hee), Earl Simmons (Bruce King), Frank
Smith (Foo Shai), William T. Dyer (the captain),
Paul Panzer (Mr Demarest), Isabel Patterson (his
wife), William Garwood (Lawrence Demarest),
Paddy Sullivan (Mike), Guy Morville (the detec-
tive), Charles Fang (Chang).*
Released: USA 3.7.16
Length: five reels

Mignon, daughter of the American consul in
Hong Kong, is adopted by a wealthy Chinese
mandarin when her only surviving parent dies.
Years later she prays to her favourite joss that she
may be allowed to go to America. She is observed
by the American trader, Foo Shai, and he leads
her through the city gate towards the sea beyond
which, he tells her, lies America. Soon she is
a captive in the New York home of the villainous
Foo Shai, 'dealer in merchandise and souls'.
But she is rescued by a young artist and finds
love and happiness at last.

THE CHALICE OF SORROW (1916)

pc: Universal-Bluebird Photoplays Inc
dir and sc: Rex Ingram
ph: B. C. (Duke) Hayward
lp: *Cleo Madison (Lorelei), Blanche White
(Isabel Clifford), Charles Cummings (Marion
Leslie), John McDermott (Rance Clifford),
Wedgewood Nowell (Francisco de Scarpina),
Howard Crampton (Siestra), Albert McQuarrie
(Pietro), Thea Maines (his wife)*
Released: USA 9.10.16
Length: five reels
English title: *The Fatal Promise*

Scarpina, governor of a Mexican province and a
monster of cruelty, covets the singer Lorelei,
betrothed to the sculptor Marion Leslie. The
latter has shielded an enemy of Scarpina's and is
imprisoned. Lorelei offers herself to Scarpina
and he signs passports to enable her and her lover
to escape over the border, whereupon she stabs
him. She watches the soldiers fire on her lover
with rifles which she has been led to believe will
contain blank cartridges. When the soldiers
depart she rushes forward only to find her lover
dead and the vengeance of the dead Scarpina
triumphant.

BLACK ORCHIDS (1916)

pc: Universal-Bluebird Photoplays Inc
dir and sc: Rex Ingram
ph: B. C. (Duke) Hayward
lp: prologue: *Cleo Madison (Marie de Severac), Francis McDonald (George Renoir), Richard la Reno (Emile le Reno)*
lp: the play: *Cleo Madison (Zoraide), Wedgewood Nowell (Marquis de Chantal), Howard Crampton (Baron de Maupin), Francis McDonald (Ivan, his son), John George (Ali Bara), Joe Martin (Haitim-Tai), Jean Hersholt (small part)*
Released: USA 1.1.17
Length: five reels

Marie de Severac, a frivolous girl, is addicted to flirting and is unhelpful to her fiancée, the artist George Renoir. Her father reads her his new novel as a warning to her to mend her ways.

Sebastian de Maupin, diplomat and roué, discovers Zoraide, a mystic prophetess in love with his son, Ivan. Zoraide encourages both father and son, but the latter has to leave for the front without having a chance to say goodbye, whereupon Zoraide consoles herself with the Marquis de Chantal, a widower and invalid to whom she was introduced by Sebastian. The latter, now jealous of the de Chantal, plans to poison him, but Zoraide's pet ape switches glasses and Sebastian himself dies. Ivan returns and is furious to find Zoraide married to de Chantal, but she contrives a duel between the two men, knowing that Ivan is the better swordsman. De Chantal is seriously wounded and, aware of his wife's unfaithfulness, arranges a mock funeral for himself and contrives an assignation between his wife and Ivan at his chateau. She is thrown into the dungeon and the dead body of her lover flung to her. His vengeance accomplished, de Chantal dies.

In an epilogue, Marie is overcome by the moral of the tale and seeks her lover's forgiveness.

THE REWARD OF THE FAITHLESS (1917)

pc: Universal-Bluebird Photoplays Inc
dir and sc: Rex Ingram
st: E. Magnus Ingleton
ph: Ralph Perry
lp: *Claire Du Brey (Princess Dione), Richard le Reno (Prince Paul Ragusin), Nicholas Dunaew (Feodor Strogoff), Wedgewood Nowell (Guido Campanelli), William J. Dyer (Peter Vlasoff), Betty Schade (Anna, his daughter), Jim Brown (Karl), Bill Rathbone (a cripple).*
Released: USA 12.2.17
Length: five reels
English title: *The Ruling Passion*

A drama of Russian life. An adventurer worms his way into the family of a wealthy nobleman and on his death marries the heiress, although she had been promised to a worthy poet. This doting woman innocently takes into her household as a maid a girl who had been betrayed by the adventurer. He now makes another bid for the maid and plots with her to remove his wife. The latter, to all appearances dead, is discovered by the poet to be in a trance. Her persuades her to allow herself to be buried in the family vault and to trust him to bring vengeance on the guilty. The funeral takes place, the poet enters the vault, revives his beloved and flees with her to Italy. After many years the adventurer and the maid visit that country. Not recognising his former wife, he is attracted by her. She plans revenge and pretends she wants the ring which his wife used to wear. She returns with him to Russia and he attempts to get the ring from the vault where he thinks his wife is buried. But it is empty and he now sees what he thinks is his wife's spirit. It advances towards him driving him slowly to a sea-cliff's edge from which he falls to his death.

THE PULSE OF LIFE (1917)

pc: Universal-Bluebird Photoplays Inc
dir and sc: Rex Ingram
st: E. Magnus Ingleton
ph: B. C. (Duke) Hayward
lp: *Gypsy Harte (Lisetta Maseto), Dorothy Barrett (Buckety Sue), Molly Malone (Molly Capels), Nicholas Dunaew (Domenic), Wedgewood Nowell (Guido Serrani), Millard K. Wilson (Stanford Graham), Albert McQuarrie (Dago Joe), Edward Brown (Luigo Maseto), Seymour Hastings (Hasting Capels)*
Released: USA 9.4.17
Length: five reels

Lisetta, a daughter of the fisherman Luigi Maseto from Capri, dreams of far-off lands and tires of her narrow environment. When Serrani, an Italian artist living in New York, is attracted by her he easily persuades her to come to New York with him, but once there he tires of her and she comes under the influence of Dago Joe, a frequenter of cafes. As a dancer she is seen by Graham, a sculptor, who gets her to pose for him. Eventually they fall in love. In the meantime Domenic, Lisetta's brother, hearing of her betrayal by Serrani, comes to New York and kills the latter with a knife lying on his desk. The ownership of the knife is traced to Graham, whose quarrel with Serrani over Lisetta is known. Graham's execution is stayed, however, by the conscience-stricken Domenic, who hands himself up to justice. Lisetta, disillusioned with New York, returns to Capri where she is joined by Dominic who has served a prison sentence for his crimes.

THE FLOWER OF DOOM (1917)

pc: Universal-Bluebird Photoplays Inc
dir, sc and st: Rex Ingram
ph: B. C. (Duke) Hayward
lp: *Yvette Mitchell (Tea Rose), Wedgewood Nowell (Sam Savinsky), Nicholas Dunaew (Paul Rasnov), Millard K. Wilson (Harvey Pearson), Gypsy Harte (Neva Sacon), Tommy Morrissey (Buck), Frank Tokonaga (Charles Sing), Gordon Keene (Ah Wong), Evelyn Selbie (Arn Fun)*
Released: USA 16.4.17
Length: five reels

At a meeting of the Hop Sing Tong a Chinese is deputed to kill a fellow-countryman. This he does. The police are diverted from tracking the criminal and arrest Charley Sing who, however, is released at the request of Buck Mahoney, a gang leader.

Samuel Savinsky, a married pawnbroker, is carrying on an intrigue with Neva Sacon and is jealous of Harvey Wilson, a reporter. Paul Rasnov, a sculptor, pawns trinkets in order to get opium from Ah Wong, leader of the Three Brothers Tong. Tea Rose, Ah Wong's wife agrees to run away with Paul.

Buck Mahoney promises to reveal the secret of Chinatown to Harvey Wilson if he will expose the Boss in his paper. Harvey is led into the headquarters of the Hop Sing Tong where he admires and steals a silver poppy — The Flower of Doom, which he presents to the cafe dancer Neva Sacon. Next day Harvy and Neva dine at Ah Wong's store. Ah Wong abducts Neva while Harvey is in another room and Harvey goes to tell Buck of the strange disappearance.

Neva bribes a Chinese guard to deliver a message to Harvey. The messenger is given a curious ring which she received from Savinsky. Harvey is not at his office and the Chinaman takes the ring to Savinsky's pawnshop. The Chinaman is forced to confess how he got the ring. Accompanied by a policeman Savinsky sets out for Ah Tong's but does not remain for the dénouement. Buck asks Charley Sing to find Neva and they capture Tea Rose and arrange an exchange of Tea Rose for Neva.

Savinsky realises he has lost Neva and demands the return of jewels he has given her but Harvey throws him out and becomes engaged to Neva.

Ah Wong frustrates a plan of Rasnov and Tea Rose to run away and he strangles his wife but is accidentally killed in a fight with Rasnov who now consoles himself with opium.

THE LITTLE TERROR (1917)

pc: Universal-Bluebird Photoplays Inc
dir and sc: Rex Ingram
ph: Harry W. Forbes
lp: *Ned Finlay (John Saunders), Violet Mersereau,*
(Tina and Alice), Robert Clugston (Wallace Saunders), Sidney Mason (George Reynolds), Jack Raymond (Archibald Watkins), Mrs Brundage (Mrs Watkins), Edward Porter (the manager)
Released: USA 30.7.17
Length: five reels

Alice is the daughter of Prince Wallace, a circus actor who had married the circus queen, Tina, against his father's wishes. When he dies Alice is adopted by her grandfather and goes to live in his mansion where she causes trouble with her pet pig and with her determination to get rid of a governess she does not like. She tries to find one more tractable.

George, a lightning artist of the circus, had always loved Alice and having become successful he returns to claim her. The grandfather taking him for a fortune-hunter, tries to get rid of him but Alice and he elope and get married, returning after the ceremony to explain to the old man that George is now earning £1,000 a week. All ends happily.

2 Two films for Paralta-W. W. Hodkinson

HIS ROBE OF HONOUR (1917)

pc: Paralta-W. W. Hodkinson Corp
dir: Rex Ingram
sc: Julian Louis Lamothe
st: Ethel and James Dorrance
ph: Carl Widem
lp: *Henry B. Walthall (Julian Randolph), Mary Charleson (Roxana Frisbee), Lois Wilson (Laura Nelson), Noah Berry ('Boss' Nordhoff), Joseph J. Dowling (Bruce Nelson), Ray Laidlaw (Robert Partland), Fred Montague (Million Mulligan), Eugene Pallette (Clifford Nordhoff), Guy Newhard (Carrots)*
Released: USA 15.1.18
Length: seven reels

Randolph, a shady lawyer, manipulates juries and witnesses. He rehearses his witnesses who are to perjure themselves for a price. He fixes his client Million Mulligan with a fiancée, his assistant Roxana. He is chivalrous enough however to rescue Laura, niece of a wealthy magnate, Nelson, from a purse snatcher. He intends to fleece Nelson and is bought off for a very solid retainer. Nordhoff, a political gangster, has a brother Clifford who shot a man and is arrested through the action of Roxana. Roxana is in love with Randolph but he loves Laura and must do some social climbing and whitewashing of himself to win her. Nordhoff engages Randolph to defend his brother and promises him a judgeship of the High Court. Randolph wins the case by his usual crooked methods and earns the reward. Randolph discovers that Roxana is a former wife of Nordhoff and he settles her on Mulligan. There is further trouble between Randolph and Nelson and eventually Randolph redeems himself. He marries Laura who invests him with his robe of honour.

HUMDRUM BROWN (1918)

pc: Paralta-W. W. Hodkinson Corp
dir: Rex Ingram
sc: R. B. Kidd
st: H. B. and M. H. Daniel
ph: Clyde R. Cook
lp: *Henry B. Walthall (Humdrum Brown), Mary Charleson (Alicia Booth), Dorothy Love Clarke (Grace Danforth), Howard Crampton (Carlos Tanner), Kate Price (Cousin Kate), Joseph J. Dowling (John Freyeburg), Joe Harris (Ed Danforth), Ida Lewis (Aunt Elvira).*
Released: USA 15.3.18
Length: five reels

Humdrum Brown, a bank clerk in the sleepy town of Norwalk, dreams of married bliss with Alicia Booth. A burglary takes place at the bank which is forced to close its doors. Going to the big city Brown gets a job as night-clerk at a hotel. Alicia, left a fortune by a rejected lover, comes to the city to invest her money in a shady enterprise managed by two crooks who live at the hotel where Humdrum works. An accomplice splits on the crooks who had robbed the bank and Humdrum chases them to a liner on which a fight takes place. The loot is captured and Humdrum becomes president of the bank.

3   Two further films for Universal

THE DAY SHE PAID (1919)

pc: Universal
dir: Rex Ingram
sc: Hal Headley and Clarkson Miller
st: Fannie Hurst ('Oats for the Woman')
ph: Steve Rounds
lp: *Francelia Billington (Marion Buckley), Charles Clary (Jay Rogers), Harry van Meter (Lear Kessler), Lillian Rich (Marina), Nancy Caswell (Betty), Lieutenant Marcel Drageauson (modiste assistant), Alice Taaffe (minor role)*
Released: USA 5.1.20
Length: five reels

Rogers, head of a big provincial dressmaking establishment, loves Marion, a mannequin. She had been betrayed by Kessler who runs a high-class dress-designing business. She marries Rogers and is attached to his two daughters by a previous marriage. The eldest becomes engaged to Kessler but Marion, determined to save the girl, confesses to her husband her former association with the man. She is driven from her home and becomes a reporter on the *Apparel Gazette*. She is determined to prevent her stepdaughter's marriage. An argument between herself and Kessler is overheard by Rogers and his daughter and the husband now realises how he has mis-

judged his wife. The villain receives a sound thrashing. Husband and wife are reconciled.

UNDER CRIMSON SKIES (1919)

pc: Universal-Jewel
dir: Rex Ingram
sc: Harvey Thew
st: J. G. Hawks
ph: Phil Rosen
lp: *Elmo Lincoln (Capt Yank Barston), Harry van Meter (Vance Clayton), Mabel Ballin (Helen, his wife), Nancy Caswell (Peg, their child), Frank Brownlee (Dead Sight Burke), Paul Weigel (Plum Duff Hargis), Dick la Reno (second mate), Noble Johnson (Baltimore Bucko), Beatrice Dominguez (island girl)*
Released: USA 5.7.20
Length: six reels

A brutal San Francisco skipper becomes friendly with the little daughter of a couple who are taking a cargo of pianos to a small Central American republic. The wife is asked to sing for the skipper and when one of the pianos is unpacked it is found to contain munitions which are intended for a group of revolutionaries. The skipper shoots a member of his crew whom he finds in league with the munition merchant. He is arrested on landing but escapes across the bay to a strange colony of beachcombers presided over by a drunken escaped convict. The skipper and the leader fight for supremacy but ultimately become friends and defeat the revolutionaries who are attacking the American embassy. They rescue the woman and child and the skipper is finally cleared by the confession of the dying sailor whom he had shot.

4   The films for Metro

SHORE ACRES (1920)

pc: Metro Pictures Corporation
dir and p: Rex Ingram
sc: Art Zellner based on James Herne's stage play
ph: John Seitz
ad: Jack Holden
at: D. Anthony Tauszley
ed: Grant Whytock
lp: *Alice Lake (Helen Berry), Robert Walker (Sam Warren), Edward Connelly (Nathaniel Berry), Frank Brownlee (Martin Berry), Margaret McWade (Ann Berry, Martin's wife), Joseph Kilgour (Josiah Blake), Burwell Mainrich (Young Nat)*
Released: USA 28.3.20
Length: five reels

Josiah Blake, a banker, covets the farm of Shore Acres. His clerk, Sam Warren, loves Helen Berry, the daughter of one of the two brothers who own the farm. Blake induces Helen's father, Martin

Berry, to mortgage it in order to invest in oil shares. The oil company goes bust and Blake now wants Helen as the price of his help. Sam, who has lost his job, is ordered off the farm. Nathaniel Berry, Helen's uncle, helps the lover to get away on the *Liddy Anne* where they are married by a skipper. A storm breaks out, the lovers being washed overboard and believed dead. Martin had prevented Nathaniel from attending to the lighthouse lantern and is stricken with remorse. But Sam and Helen are washed ashore alive. Blake tries to have Sam arrested for theft but is himself brought to justice and all ends happily.

HEARTS ARE TRUMPS (1920)

pc: Metro Pictures Corporation
dir and p: Rex Ingram
sc: June Mathis, based on the play by Cecil Raleigh
ph: John Seitz
ad: Arthur Ruoda
ed: Grant Whytock
lp: *Winter Hall (Lord Altcar), Joseph Kilgour (Lord Burford), Frank Brownlee (Michael Wain), Edward Connelly (the Abbot of St Bernard), Thomas Jefferson (Henry Dyson), Brinsley Shaw (Israel Fell), Norman Kennedy (John Gillespie), Francelia Billington (Lady Winifred), Alice Terry (Dora Woodberry)*
Released: USA 12.12.20
Length: six reels

Lord Altcar intends to trade his daughter, Lady Winifred, to Lord Burford in order to cover his losses at cards. She, however, has secretly married the gamekeeper, Michael Wain, who is horribly beaten by Altcar and driven off the estate. Years pass and Wain returns to find Lady Winifred the owner of Altcar Manor to which he had bought the mortgages. He intends to foreclose when unexpected events occur. Lady Winifred has a daughter, brought up in Switzerland, who is now restored to her mother.

The girl, Dora, engaged to an American artist, Gillespie, attracts the attentions of the same Lord Burford who once wished to marry her mother. Burford manages to obtain a painting of the girl and alters the body to a nude just before its exhibition. The girl, mortified by what she thinks is her lover's insensitiveness, runs away to a convent in the Swiss Alps. At the exhibition her father reveals his identity and he and Lady Winifred are reconciled. Burford, through an accomplice, finds out Dora's destination and gets there before her and has her brought to his chalet. Wain and Lady Winifred are in hot pursuit. The girl struggles for freedom and Burford is killed by his accomplice, Felder, from motives of revenge. Felder seeks to possess the girl who tears off his glasses, blinding him, and escaping into the storm where she is found by her father, mother and lover. Felder is killed in the avalanche.

THE FOUR HORSEMEN OF THE APOCALYPSE (1921)

pc: Metro Pictures Corporation
dir and p: Rex Ingram
sc: June Mathis based on the novel by Vicente Blasco Ibáñez
ph: John Seitz
asst ph: Walter Mayo; Starret Ford
ed: Grant Whytock and June Mathis
ad: Walter Mayo, Curt Rehfeld
tech asst: Amos Myers, Joseph Calder
at: John W. Robinson
lp: *Rudolph Valentino (Julio Desnoyers), Alice Terry (Marguerite Laurier), Pomeroy Cannon (Madariaga, the Centaur), Josef Swickard (Marcelo Desnoyers), Brinsley Shaw (Celendonio), Alan Hale (Karl von Hartrott), Bridgetta Clark (Dona Luisa), Mabel van Buren (Elena), Brodwich 'Smoke' Turner (Argensola), Nigel de Brulier (Tchernoff), John Sainpolis (Laurier), Mark Fenton (Senator Lacour), Virginia Warwick (Chichi), Derek Ghent (René Lacour), Stuart Holmes (Captain von Hartrott), Jean Hersholt (Professor von Hartrott), Henry Klaus (Hendrick von Hartrott), Edward Connelly (lodge-keeper), Georgia Woodthorpe (lodge-keeper's wife), Kathleen Key (Georgette), Wallace Beery (Lt.-Colonel von Richthoffen), Jacques d'Auray (Captain dAubrey), Curt Rehfeld (Major Blumhardt), Mlle Dolores (Mlle Lucette, a model), Bull Montana (the French butcher), Isabel Keith (the German woman), Jacques Lanoe (her husband), Noble Johnson (Conquest), Harry Northrup (the count), Minnehaha (the old nurse), Arthur Hoyt (Lieutenant Schnitz), Beatrice Dominguez (dancer), Apocalypse I (monkey). Jean Hersholt was also make-up man.*
Première: Lyric Theatre, New York 6.3.21
Length: eleven reels

De Madariaga, known as the Centaur, is a settler in the Argentine and the owner of vast ranches. He has two daughters, one married to a Frenchman who fled his country to escape conscription during the Franco-Prussian War, the other to a German who trains his sons in the Prussian tradition. Julio Desnoyers, the son of the Frenchman, is his grandfather's favourite, but grows up a pleasure-loving libertine. When the old man dies the two families divide the fortune between them and return to their respective countries. In Paris, Marcelo Desnoyers develops a mania for collecting antiques and buys a castle to house his treasures at Villeblanche beside the Marne. His son, Julio, sets up as an artist and one of his amorous conquests is Marguerite Laurier, the wife of one of his father's friends. Their secret is discovered and a divorce is pending when the war breaks out. Paris is in a patriotic ferment. Laurier goes to the war and Julio remains behind with his beloved until she, stricken by conscience, enlists as a nurse. In the room above Julio's studio Tchernoff, a Russian mystic evokes the vision of the Apocalyptic Horsemen who bring Conquest, Famine, War and Death. A tragedy is enacted before their eyes when the German wife of a French soldier kills herself. Meanwhile old Desnoyers goes to his castle and witnesses the destruction of the village by the German hordes and is forced to play host to the conquerors who include his nephew. On the repulsion of the Germans Desnoyers returns to Paris swearing vengeance. He is overjoyed when he learns that Julio has at last joined up. He visits the boy at the front before the big attack. Julio again meets Marguerite who is tending her blind husband at Lourdes. She, however, decides to remain with her husband who is unaware of her identity. Julio returns to the trenches and is killed, while in Berlin the German family, too, mourn the death of their sons. In a final scene in a war cemetery Julio's sister and her returned lover look to the future while the mysterious Tchernoff surveys the thousands of crosses and says 'I knew them all'.

THE CONQUERING POWER (1921)

pc: Metro Picture Corporation
dir and p: Rex Ingram
sc: June Mathis
ph: John Seitz
ed: Grant Whytock
ad: Ralph Barton and Amos Myers
lp: *Ralph Lewis (Père Grandet), Alice Terry (Eugénie Grandet), Rudolph Valentino (Charles Grandet), Carrie Daumery (Mme Grandet), Eric Mayne (Victor Grandet), Edward Connelly (Notary Cruchot), George Atkinson (Young Cruchot), Willard Lee Hall (the Abbé), Mark Fenton (M de Grassins), Bridgetta Clark (Mme de Grassins), Ward Wing (Adolph), Mary Hearn (Nanòn), Eugéne Poujet (Cornoiller), Andrée Tourneur (Annette).*
Première: Rivoli Theatre, New York, 3.7.21
Length: 7000 ft.

Père Grandet, a rich miser, lives frugally with his wife and daughter, Eugénie, in a cottage. His ruined brother sends his socialite son Charles, to Grandet and then commits suicide. Charles, now penniless, is forced by Grandet to sign over his father's estate and departs for Martinique with the help of savings given by his cousin Eugénie who loves him. Grandet intercepts Charles's letters to Eugénie and tells him that she is to be married. Eugénie however resists her suitors, who are after her inheritance and one day finds a letter of Charles's in a cellar. Escaping from her father she locks him in his strong room. He is haunted by terrible delusions and goes mad. A heavy chest of gold falls on him and kills him. Charles returns in time to rescue Eugénie from further persecution and marries her.

TURN TO THE RIGHT (1921)

pc: Metro Picture Corporation
dir and p: Rex Ingram
sc: Mary O'Hara, June Mathis
ph: John Seitz
ed: Grant Whytock
asst d: Curt Rehfeld
tech assts: Amos Myers, Harold Grieve
lp: *Lydia Knott (Mrs Bascom), Jack Mulhall (Joe Bascom), Betty Allen (Betty Bascom), Edward Connelly (Deacon Tillinger), Alice Terry (Elsie Tillinger), William Bletcher (Sam Martin), Harry Myers (Gilly), George Cooper (Muggs), Margaret Loomis (Jessie Strong), Eric Mayne (Mr Morgan), Ray Ripley (Lester Morgan)*
Première: Lyric Theatre, New York 23.1.22
Length: 7703 ft

Joe Bascom, in love with Elsie, daughter of Deacon Tillinger, leaves his native village to seek his fortune. He becomes a groom at a racing stable, but is imprisoned on a charge put up by his employer's son. Meanwhile two fellow prisoners who manage to steal money from Tillinger to pay off loans for Joe's mother. The man who framed Joe is unmasked and his former employer gives him back with interest the money he was supposed to have stolen. With this Joe turns his mother's farm into a prosperous jam-making enterprise and marries Elsie. His two friends marry women from the village.

THE PRISONER OF ZENDA (1922)

pc: Metro Pictures Corporation
dir and p: Rex Ingram
sc: Mary O'Hara, based on Edward Rose's stage adaptation of Anthony Hope's novel
ph: John Seitz
ed: Grant Whytock
asst ed: Curt Rehfeld
ad: Amos Myers
tech assts: Harold Grieve, Jack W Robson
lp: *Lewis Stone (Rudolph Rassendyll and Rudolph V of Ruritania), Alice Terry (Princess Flavia), Robert Edeson (Colonel Sapt), Stuart Holmes (Black Michael), Ramon Samaniegos (Rupert of Hentzau), Malcolm McGregor (Fritz von Tarlenheim), Barbara La Marr (Antoinette de Mauban), Edward Connelly (Marshal Strakenc), Lois Lee (Countess Helga), John George (the Lizard), Thur Fairfax (Bersonin), Al Jennings (De Gautet), F. G. Becker (Detchard), Snitz Edwards (Josef), Harry Jones (Hans).*
Première: Astor Theatre, New York 31.7.22
Length: 10,467 ft

Rudolph Rassendyll, hearing of the approaching coronation of a relation of his in Ruritania, leaves his English home to go hunting in that country. Rudolph, the king-to-be, is weak and dissipated and plans to spend the days prior to the coronation at Zenda, the hunting-lodge of his half-brother Black Michael who covets the throne. Here he is drugged and Rasendyll, having stumbled into the scene, is persuaded by the King's friends to impersonate him at the ceremony and so foil Black Michael's plot. On the day, he meets Princess Flavia, the King's betrothed, who finds an unfamiliar sympathy with the man she is to wed but she does not suspect the deception. The King is prisoner at Black Michael's castle at Zenda and when Michael hears through his agent, Antoinette de Mauban, of the trick played on him he plots with his henchman, Rupert of Hentzau, to assassinate Rassendyll. The marriage of the King and Flavia is announced, the attempt on Rassendyll's life is foiled, and the King is rescued. But Flavia and Rassendyll must part since they place their sense of duty above personal feelings.

TRIFLING WOMEN (1922)

pc: Metro Pictures Corporation
dir and p: Rex Ingram
sc: Rex Ingram (from his own story *Black Orchids*)
ph: John Seitz
prod man: Starrett Ford
ed: Grant Whytock
tech assts: Jean de Limur and Robert Florey
ad: Leo Kuter
lp: *Pomeroy Cannon (Léon de Séverac), Barbara La Marr (Jacqueline and Zareda), Ramon Novarro (Henri and Ivan), Edward Connelly (Baron de Maupin), Lewis Stone (the Marquis Ferroni), Hughie Mack (innkeeper), John George (Achmet), Jesse Weldon (Caesar), Hyman Binunsky (Hassan), Eugéne Poujet (the valet), Joe Martin (the secret agent — an ape).*
Première: Astor Theatre, New York, 2.10.22
Length: 8,800 ft

Zareda, a Parisian crystal gazer, attracts the decrepit Baron de Maupin and his son Ivan. When Ivan goes off to the war, the father throws Zareda into the arms of the wealthy Marquis Ferroni. But when he plans to poison the Marquis he himself dies when the cups are switched by Zareda's familiar ape. When Ivan returns from the war he finds Zareda married to the Marquis. Zareda, however, loves Ivan and arranges that he shall fight her husband in a duel during which the Marquis is supposedly mortally wounded. He survives long enough to arrange a mock funeral and to entrap the lovers in the dungeon of the Sorcerer's Tower where Zareda is buried alive beside the body of her dead lover. This Gothic tale has both a prologue and epilogue and is given as a novelist's warning to his flirtatious daughter.

WHERE THE PAVEMENT ENDS (1923)

pc: Metro Pictures Corporation
dir and p: Rex Ingram
sc: Rex Ingram (from *The Passion Vine* in John Russell's book of short stories *Where the Pavement Ends*)
ph: John Seitz
ed: Grant Whytock
tech assts: Gordon Mayer, Morton Spring, Gordon Avil
prod man: Colonel Starrett Ford
lp: *Edward Connelly (Pastor Spener), Alice Terry (Matilda Spener), Ramon Novarro (Motauri), Harry T. Morey (Captain Hull Gregson), John George (Napuka Joe)*
Première: Capitol Theatre, New York, 1.4.23
Length: 7,706 ft

The Reverend Mr Spener runs a mission station on the island of Wilea where his only daughter Matilda assists him in his work. A Kanaka boy of noble heritage, Motauri, falls in love with Matilda, who is coveted by the vicious Captain Hull Gregson. The lovers are ultimately separated and Matilda returns to civilisation. Motauri kills himself in the waterfall which formed the background of their secret meetings.

SCARAMOUCHE (1923)

pc: Metro Pictures Corporation
dir and p: Rex Ingram
sc: Willis Goldbeck (from the novel by Rafael Sabatini)
ph: John Seitz
ed: Grant Whytock
tech assts: Curt Rehfeld, Amos Myers, John J. Hughes, Jack W. Robson, Arthur Smith
costumes: O'Kane Cornwell, Eve Roth, Van Horn
lp: *Ramon Novarro (André Louis Moreau), Alice Terry (Aline de Kercadiou), Lewis Stone (Marquis de la Tour d'Azyr), Lloyd Ingraham (Quentin de Kercadiou), Julia Swayne Gordon (Countess Therese de Plougastel), William Humphrey (Chevalier de Chabrillane), Otto Matiesen (Philip de Vilmorin), George Siegmann (Danton), Bowditch Turner (Chapelier), James Marcus (Binet), Edith Allen (Climene Binet), Lydia Yeamans Titus (Mme Binet), John George (Polichinelle), Nelson McDowell (Rhodomont), de Garcia Fuerburg (Robespierre), Roy Coulson (Marat), Edwin Argus (Louis XVI), Clothilde Delano (Marie Antoinette), Willard Lee Hall (the King's Lieutenant), Slavko Vorkapich (Napoleon), Lorimer Johnston (Count Dupuye), Edward Connelly (Minister to the King), Howard Gaye (Viscount d'Albert), J. Edwin Brown (M Benoit), Carrie Clark Ward (Mme Benoit), Edward Coxen (Jacques), Rose Dione (La Révolte).*
Première: 44th Street Theatre, New York, 30.9.23
Length: 9,850 ft

A young Breton law student, André Louis Moreau, joins the revolutionaries when his friend,

Philip de Vilmorin, is killed in an unfair duel by the Marquis de la Tour d'Azyr. He hides with a band of strolling players and plays the role of Scaramouche. He is in love with his godfather's daughter, Aline de Kercadiou. She, however, is attracted by the Marquis and André Louis becomes engaged to Climène, an actress, only to learn she is the Marquis's mistress. Aline also finds out about this and now realises that she loves André Louis who has become a People's Deputy in the Government and also a famous duellist. He defeats in a duel the proud Marquis who has been killing the people's leaders in duels which he had deliberately provoked. The Revolution has succeeded, but Aline and her aunt being aristocrats are in grave danger when they are trapped in Paris. André Louis, however, helps them to escape and leaves with them. He learns that the Marquis is in fact his own father. The Marquis dies at the hands of the mob, cynical but courageous to the end.

THE ARAB (1924)

pc: Metro-Goldwyn
dir and p: Rex Ingram
sc: Rex Ingram (adapted from the stage play by Edgar Selwyn)
ph: John Seitz
ed: Grant Whytock
tech assts: John Birkel, George Noffka, Curt Rehfeld, F. Medelgi, Jean de Limur
lp: *Ramon Novarro (Jamil), Alice Terry (Mary Hilbert), Jerrold Robertshaw (Dr Hilbert), Maxudian (the Governor), Jean de Limur (Hossein), Adelqui Millar (Abdullah), Paul Vermoyal (Iphraim), Justa Uribe (Myrza), Giuseppe de Campo (Selim), Paul Francesci (Marmont), Alexandresco (an Ouled Naïl)*
Première: Capitol Theatre, New York, 13.7.24
Length: 6,710 ft.

Mary Hilbert, a missionary's daughter, tries to convert Jamil, the son of a Bedouin chief. They are mutually attracted. The Governor of the province seeks the aid of Jamil's father in a plot to massacre the Christians. Failing to obtain this ally, he plans to kill a group of Christian children and persuades Mary that Jamil's tribe are the villains. Jamil learns of this deception but Mary will not trust him. He saves the children and his father comes at the head of his followers to capture the Governor. Jamil returns to his people, but Mary begs his forgiveness and hints that she will return to him after she has made a visit to England.

MARE NOSTRUM (1925-6)

pc: Metro-Goldwyn
dir and p: Rex Ingram
sc: Willis Goldbeck (based on the novel by Vicente Blasco Ibáñez)

ph: John Seitz
ed: Grant Whytock
tech assts: Harry Lachman, George Noffka, Joseph Boyle, John Birkel, Walter Palmer
lp: *Uni Apollon (the Triton), Alex Nova (Don Esteban Ferragut), Kada Abd-el-Kader (Ulysses, his son, as a boy), Hughie Mack (Caragol), Alice Terry (Freya Talberg), Antonio Moreno (Ulysses Ferragut), Mlle Kithnou (his wife, Dona Cinta), Mickey Brantford (their son Esteban), Rosita Ramirez (their niece Pepita), Frederick Mariotti (Toni, the mate), Madame Paquerette (Dr Feldmann), Fernand Mailly (Count Kaledine), André von Engelmann (submarine commander)*.
Première: Criterion Theatre, New York, 15.2.26
Length: 11,000 ft, later cut to 9,894 ft

Ulysses Ferragut, of a sea-going family from Barcelona, decides to give up his calling to settle down with his wife and son. But the possibility of earning money with his boat the *Mare Nostrum*, now that war has broken out, proves too great a temptation. At Naples an attractive woman, Freya, persuades him to supply oil to the German submarines in the Mediterranean. His young son, coming to Naples to persuade him to return home, is on a ship sunk by a submarine. Ulysses swears vengeance against those he had previously helped. Freya, betrayed by her own organisation, is captured by the French and shot as a spy. Ulysses sinks the German vessel which caused his son's death, but he and his ship, the *Mare Nostrum*, are swallowed up by the waters which re-unit him mystically with Freya who has come to symbolise the goddess Amphitrite.

THE MAGICIAN (1926)

pc: Metro-Goldwyn
dir and p: Rex Ingram
sc: Rex Ingram (adapted from W. Somerset Maugham's novel)
ph: John Seitz
ed: Grant Whytock
ad: Henri Menessier
tech assts: Harry Lachman and George Noffka
lp: *Alice Terry (Margaret Dauncey), Paul Wegener (Oliver Haddo), Firmin Gemier (Doctor Porhoet), Ivan Petrovitch (Arthur Burdon), Gladys Hamer (Susie Boyd), Henry Wilson (Haddo's servant), Stowitts (dancing faun)*.
Première: Capitol Theatre, New York, 24.10.26
Length: 6,960 ft

Oliver Haddo, madman and magician, hypnotises Margaret Dauncey and takes her away on the eve of her marriage to Dr Arthur Burdon who has saved her life by a skilful operation. His plan is to use, as per an ancient formula, her virgin's heart to infuse life into an inanimate body. Dr Burdon pursues them and gets her away but ultimately Haddo lures her to his lonely laboratory tower on the edge of a precipice. Just as he is about to perform his evil operation,

Arthur arrives and rescues her. The tower, and Haddo with it, is destroyed by fire.

THE GARDEN OF ALLAH (1927)

pc: Metro-Goldwyn
dir and p: Rex Ingram
sc: Willis Goldbeck (based on the novel by Robert Hichens)
ph: Leo Garmes, Monroe Bennett, Marcel Lucien
ed: Arthur Ellis
prod man: Harry Lachman
tech asst: John Birkel
ad: Henri Menessier
lp: *Alice Terry (Dominie Enfilden), Ivan Petrovitch (Father Adrian, Boris Androvsky), Marcel Vibert (Count Anteoni), H. Humberston Wright (Lord Rens), Mme Paquerette (Suzanne), Gerald Fielding (Batouche), H. Dutertre (the Priest of Beni-Mora), Ben Sadour (the sand diviner), Claude Fielding (Hadj), Rehba Ben Salah (Ayesha), Michael Powell (a tourist).*
Première: Embassy Theatre, New York, 2.9.27
Length: 8,500 ft

In North Africa a Trappist monk, Boris Androvsky, breaks his vows and flees to the desert. He meets a young girl, Dominie Enfilden, who has come to seek peace and consolation. They fall in love and he marries her. Oppressed with guilt he realises that if Dominie knew about his past she would regard the marriage as a sacrilege. While they are encamped in the desert a fierce storm threatens them. Boris prays for the life of his wife and promises to give her up if they are saved. When they are rescued, he reveals his secret. She accepts the sacrifice he must make and he returns to the monastery. She remains with the consolation of her faith and the child she bears to Boris.

5 Last films

THE THREE PASSIONS (1929)

pc: St George's Productions Ltd
dir and p: Rex Ingram
sc: Rex Ingram (based on a novel by Cosmo Hamilton)
ph: L. H. Burel
ad: Henri Menessier
ed: Arthur Ellis
at: Cosmo Hamilton
lp: *Alice Terry (Lady Victoria Burlington, 'Blossy'), Shayle Gardner (Viscount Bellamont), Ivan Petrovitch (Philip Wrexham, his son), Leslie Faber (Father Aloysius), Andrews Engelmann (the hairless man), Claire Eames (Lady Bellamont), Gerald Fielding (Bobbie), Rosita Ramirez (the girl in the restaurant)*
Première: Jamaica Cinema, Long Island, 28.4.29 (the following day opened at Loew's Metropolitan

Theatre, New York City)
Length: 7,576 ft in silent version
6,646 ft in a part-talking version.
Viscount Bellamont, self-made master of one of the world's great shipyards, is bitterly disappointed when his son Philip returns from Oxford to join the Anglican Brotherhood. So is 'Blossy', Lady Victoria Burlington, who is in love with him and has shared his youthful escapades. She finds out that he works at a seaman's mission and enrols as a voluntary helper, hoping to win him back. Philip rescues her from an attack by a brutal sailor and declares his love. Bellamont, disappointed not only in his son, has also to endure the infidelities of his pleasure-loving wife. A strike at the shipyard is the last straw to the old man. Philip and 'Blossy' visit him to find him dying, but he lives long enough to learn that his son has persuaded the men to return to work and is ready to step into his father's shoes as manager of the shipyard.

BAROUD (1932)

dist: Gaumont British Corporation
dir: Rex Ingram and Alice Terry
p: Rex Ingram
sc: Rex Ingram and Peter Spencer (based on a story by Rex Ingram and Benno Vignay)
ph: L. H. Burel, P. Portier, A. Allgeier, Marcel Lucien, T. Tomatis
ad: Henri Menessier and Jean Lafitte
ed: Lothar Wolff
mus dir: Louis Levy
sd: RCA
lp: *Felipe Montes (Si Allal, Caid of Ilouet), Rosita Garcia (Zinah, his daughter), Pierre Batcheff (Si Hamed, his son and sergeant of the Corps of Spahis), Rex Ingram (André Duval, a sergeant of the corps of Spahis), Arabella Fields (Mabrouka, a slave), Andrews Engelmann (Si Amarok, a bandit chief), Dennis Hoey (Captain Labry), Laura Salerni (Arlette).*
Released in Great Britain 22.2.33
Released in USA under title *Love in Morocco* 20.3.33
Length: 7,265 ft

André Duval and Si Hamed are officers in a Spahi regiment. When Si Hamed discovers that his friend is in love with his sister, Zinah, he feels obliged by Moorish custom to kill the infidel. Si Hamed is the son of a Berber chieftain who is involved in a tribal war with the bandit Si Amarok. The latter plans to marry Zinah and make a bogus treaty with Si Allal, her father, but his treachery is discovered and Duval and the Spahis defend Si Allal's casbah against the bandit hordes. A more sympathetic atmosphere is thus created for the course of true love. In the end Zinah waves farewell to her lover as he rides off with the Spahi regiment.

Sources and Acknowledgements

This book could not have been written without the valuable help of many people and much research into the records of the past. The principal sources of the book are indicated here and my sincere thanks must go to those who gave willingly their time and knowledge.

1   Correspondents and People Interviewed

The late Garry Alderson, London
Bruce Allan, Edinburgh
The late James Anderson, London
The Rev Mr Frank Argyll, St Colomba's College, Dublin
Mme la Comtesse Armand d'Aix, Nice
Paul Ballard, Los Angeles
Barry Bernard, New Orleans
Mlle Dagmar Bolin, Paris
Mrs Eileen Bowser, Museum of Modern Art, New York
Kevin Brownlow, London
Leonce-Henry Burel, Mougins
George Busby, London
James Card, Rochester, New York
M. Clair, Victorine Studios, Nice
Thomas Quinn Curtiss, Paris
Miss Brenda Davies, British Film Institute, London
C. M. Dobbs, Old Columban Society, Dublin
Harold Dunham, London
Mme Lotte Eisner, Paris
Andrews Engelmann, Basle
Leslie Flint, London
The late Myrtil Frida, Prague
George Geltzer, New York
Mrs Cherrie Gill, Dublin
Mrs Lewis Way Graves, Dillsburg, Pennsylvania
The late Dr Kenneth Greer, Stoughton
Major R. D. Greer, Dublin
W. B. Hill, Santa Monica, California
The late Lt-Colonel F. C. Hitchcock, MC, OBE, Beaconsfield
John Kobal, London
Harry Lachman, Aix-en-Provence
The late Lee Lawrie, Easton, Maryland
M Jacques Ledoux, Cinémathèque Royal de Belgique, Brussels
Miss Betty Leese, British Film Institute, London
The late Jean Comte de Limur, Paris
The late Canon Britain de G. Lockheed, Kinnitty
Captain Alistair McIntosh, Monte Carlo
The late Miss Cleo Madison, Burbank, California
C. A. Maitland, MGM, London
Metro-Goldwyn-Mayer Pictures Ltd, Hollywood, California
The Reverend Mr Anthony Moore, Eastleigh
George Morrison, Dublin
Dr Henry L. Mueller, Urbana, Illinois
Jack Mulhall, Hollywood, California
Amleto Negri, Nice
The late Ramon Novarro, Hollywood, California
Miquel Porter-Moix, Barcelona
M. Pouchet, Paris
Michael Powell, London
George Pratt, George Eastman House, Rochester, New York
René Prédal, Nice
Edward Quinn, Nice
The Rank Organisation, London
Representative Body of the Church of Ireland, Dublin
The late John F. Seitz, Hollywood, California
Frederick L. Sexton, New Haven, Connecticut
Anthony Slide, Los Angeles, California
James Sloane, London
Mrs Adelaide Sparrow, Dublin
Mrs Alice Terry-Ingram, Hollywood, California
Reinhold Thiel, Berlin
The late Miss Nora Traylen, British Film Institute, London
The late Frank Tuttle, Hollywood, California
Universal Pictures Co Inc, Universal City, California
James Ursini, Los Angeles, California
Max de Vaucorbeil, Paris
Mme Denise Vernac, Maurepas
Miss Elizabeth Waggoner, Hollywood, California
Herman Weinberg, New York

2   Books

American Film Institute. *Feature Films 1921-30* 2 vols (New York, 1971)
Bennett, Alfred Gordon. *Cinemania* (London, 1937)
Benton, Thomas Hart. *An Artist in America* (New York, 1937)
Brownlow, Kevin. *The Parade's Gone By* (London, 1968)
Bulfin, William. *Rambles in Eirinn* (Dublin, 1907)
Florey, Robert. *Filmland* (Paris, 1923)
        Hollywood d'Hier et Aujourd'hui (Paris, 1948)
Freeburg, Victor Oscar. *Art of Photoplay Making* (USA, 1918)
        Pictorial Beauty on the Screen (New York, (1923)
Goldwyn, Sam. *Behind the Screen* (London, 1924)
Hamilton, Cosmo. *Underwritten History* (London, 1924)
Higham, Charles. *Hollywood Cameramen* (London, 1970)
Hitchcock, Reverend Francis Ryan Montgomery. *The Midland Septs and the Pale* (Dublin, 1908)
Ingram, Rex. *The Legion Advances* (London, 1934)
        Mars in the House of Death (New York, 1939; London, 1940)
Lowry, Caroline. *The First 100 Noted Men and Women of the Screen* (New York, 1920)
Maxwell, Gavin. *Lords of the Atlas* (London, 1966)

Milne, Peter. *Motion Picture Directing* (New York, 1922)
Photoplay Research Society. *Opportunities in the Motion Picture* (Los Angeles, 1922)
Predal, Rene, *Rex Ingram* (Paris, 1970)
Ramsaye, Terry. *A Million and One Nights* (New York, 1926)
Scully, Frank. *Cross My Heart* (New York, 1955)
Sherwood, Robert. *The Best Movie Pics of 1922-23* (Boston, 1924)
Stokes, Sewell. *Pilloried* (New York, 1929)
A Topographical History of Ireland, 2 Vols (London, 1837)
Wakhevitch, Georges. *L'Envers Des Decors* (Paris, 1977)

3 Main Articles

Atkinson, G. A. 'Rex Ingram Becomes a Mahommedan', *Daily Express* (20 May 1927)
    'Rex Ingram Makes a Full Confession', *Daily Express* (19 December 1927)
    'I Discover What's Wrong with the Talkies', *Sunday Chronicle* (2 Ocber 1932)
Bodeen, De Witt. 'Rex Ingram and Alice Terry'. *Films in Review* (February & March 1975)
Costa, Gabriel. 'Rex Ingram – A New Hero', *Film Pictorial* (15 October 1932)
Davidson, H. S. 'Rex Ingram Visited', *Picturegoer* (December 1927)
Geltzer, George. 'Hollywood's Handsomest Director', *Films in Review* (May 1952)
Goldbeck, Willis. 'Pliant Clay', *Motion Picture Classic* (March 1922)
Hall, Gladys. 'Inside with the Ingrams', *Motion Picture Magazine* (July 1927)
Hersholt, Jean. 'Memoirs' *Screen Pictorial* (Nov. 1938-Jan. 1939)
Howes, H. 'How He Makes Them Act', *Photoplay* (December 1922)
Ingram, Rex. 'On Acting', *Photoplay Magazine* (June 1923)
    'How I Look at Life', *Daily Express* (28 June 1927)
    'Art Advantages of the European Scene', *Theatre Magazine* (January 1928)
    'Silent Pictures are Finished – And a Good Thing Too', *Evening Standard* (27 April 1929)
Lederer, Josie P. 'Rex and Regina', *Pictures and Picturegoer* (December 1923)
O'Connor, Rt Hon T. P. 'Rex Ingram, the Great Producer and His Methods', *Daily Mail* (11 and 15 March 1926)
Pratt, George. 'If You Beat Me I Wept', *Image* (March 1973)
Robinson, John. 'Traditions? Never Heard of Them', *Photoplay* (August 1921)
Sheridan, Oscar. 'Why Rex Ingram Ran Away from Hollywood', *Screenland* (March 1933)
Sherwood, Robert E. '*The Four Horsemen of the Apocalypse'*, *Look* (24 April 1921)
de Somacarrers, Manuel P. 'Cuando Rex Ingram Hacer de Niza un Hollywood Europeo', *Otro Cinema,* Madrid (No 33, 1958)
Terry, Alice, 'What is Love?', *Photoplay* (November 1924)
Turner, W. B. 'The Omegas of Ingram', *Picturegoer* (July 1925)

4 Newspaper and Journals

GREAT BRITAIN
The Bioscope
Close Up
Film Pictorial
Film Weekly
Illustrated London News
Kinematograph Weekly
Picturegoer
Picture Show
Screenland
The Sketch
The Tatler
The Times

USA
American Theatre Magazine
Dramatic Index
Dramatic Review
Films in Review
Motion Picture Classic
Motion Picture Magazine
Motion Picture News
Movie Home Journal
Moving Picture World
Movie Weekly
New York Herald Tribune
New York Times
Photoplay
Picture Stories Magazine
Universal News
Variety

5 Film Archives

Academy of Motion Picture Arts and Science, Los Angeles
American Film Institute, Los Angeles
British Film Institute, London
Cinémathèque Francaise, Paris
Cinémathèque Royale de Belgique, Brussels
Czechoslovak Film Archive, Prague
Det Danske Film Museum, Copenhagen
George Eastman House, Rochester, New York
Museum of Modern Art, New York

6 Illustrations

Illustrations have been provided by Mrs Alice Terry-Ingram, the late Lt-Colonel Frank C. Hitchcock, MC, OBE, Mrs Cherrie Gill, many film archives and the John Kobal and Kevin Brownlow Collections.
    Film scenes are by courtesy of Metro-Goldwyn-Mayer, International Universal, Twentieth-Century Fox, Warner Brothers and the Rank Organisation.

7 Technical Assistance

The author wishes to thank all who have contributed to this book and to the following who have rendered valuable technical assistance: Eddie McEvoy and Phil Dowling of Radio Telefis Eireann's Photographic Department and Miss Paula Forde of the same organisation. The encouragement and help of Olwyn Callaghan has made the appearance of this book a reality.

Index

The index does not refer to the filmography which starts on page 209.
Films are listed in a separate alphabetical sequence after proper names.

Printed by
Arti Grafiche Friulane
Udine, Italy